Leonard Wells Volk

History of the Douglas Monument at Chicago

Prefaced With a Brief Sketch of Senator Douglas' life

Leonard Wells Volk

History of the Douglas Monument at Chicago
Prefaced With a Brief Sketch of Senator Douglas' life

ISBN/EAN: 9783337014247

Printed in Europe, USA, Canada, Australia, Japan

Cover: Foto ©ninafisch / pixelio.de

More available books at **www.hansebooks.com**

HISTORY

OF THE

DOUGLAS MONUMENT

AT CHICAGO;

PREFACED WITH A

BRIEF SKETCH OF SENATOR **DOUGLAS' LIFE,**

Illustrations of the Monument, etc.

BY

LEONARD W. VOLK,

SCULPTOR, AND DESIGNER **OF THE MONUMENT.**

CHICAGO:
THE CHICAGO LEGAL NEWS COMPANY.
1880.

DOUGLAS MONUMENT.

STATUE SURMOUNTING THE MONUMENT.

CONTENTS.

	PAGE
Death of Senator Douglas, with a brief Sketch of his Life	3
The Resting-place of Douglas	9
Letter of Mrs. Adele Douglas to L. W. Volk	10
Meeting to organize the Monument Association	11
Articles of Association, with Signatures	13
Meeting of Monument Association and Election of Trustees	16
Trustees' Appeal to the People in behalf of Monument	18
Act to Incorporate the Douglas Monument Association	21
Circular addressed to Legislature by Executive Committee	24
Advertisement for Designs for Monument	25
Adoption by Trustees of Leonard W. Volk's Design	26
Bill for Appropriation to Purchase Ground	26
Report of Legislative Proceedings thereon	27
Letter of Gov. Oglesby to Mrs. Douglas	28
Report of Doings of the Association	29
Mrs. Douglas' Deed to State of Illinois	31
Laying of the Corner-stone — Letter of Invitation to and Reply of Secretary Seward	34
Comments of the "Chicago Times"	36
Letter from Gov. Oglesby	39
Explanatory Letter of Secretary of Association	40
Dispatch from Secretary Seward	44
Correspondence between Superintendent Swinyard and Secretary Seward	45
Articles deposited under Corner-stone	46
The Presidential Party at Laying of Corner-stone	47
Chief Marshal's Order of Arrangements	48

CONTENTS.

"New York Herald's" Account of the Journey of the President to Chicago and Ceremonies at the Grave	51
Oration of Gen. John A. Dix	64
Speech of President Johnson	82
Speech of Secretary Seward	83
Receipts at Laying of Corner-stone	85
Remains deposited in Sarcophagus	86
Meeting of Board of Trustees	87
Letter of Mrs. Williams, formerly Mrs. Douglas	89
Financial Statement submitted to Legislature	89
Bill for Removal of Monument	90
Bill to Appropriate $50,000 to Complete Monument, 1875	92
Bill to Appropriate $50,000 as finally passed, 1877	93
Passage of the Appropriation	94
Speech of Hon. Joseph E. Smith in House of Representatives	99
Passage of House Bill in Senate	109
Meeting of the Monument Commission	110
Agreement between Commissioners and Leonard W. Volk	112
Proposals for Granite Work	113
Agreement for Colossal Statue of Douglas	114
Unveiling of Statue and Remarks of Judge Caton	115
Agreement for four symbolical Statues, representing "Illinois," "History," "Justice" and "Eloquence"	116
Bill to Appropriate $9,000 Additional to Complete Monument, passed 1879	118
Agreement for four *Bas-reliefs*	119
Description and Dimensions of Monument as Completed, with Cost of same	120

HISTORY OF
THE DOUGLAS MONUMENT.

DEATH OF SENATOR DOUGLAS, AS ANNOUNCED IN THE CHICAGO TRIBUNE JUNE 4, 1861.

STEPHEN ARNOLD DOUGLAS, Senator in Congress from Illinois, died at the Tremont House, in this city, on Monday morning, at ten minutes past nine o'clock, after a painful illness of somewhat more than a month.

The subject of the deep and universal grief which shrouds our streets, was born at Brandon, Rutland county, Vermont, April 23d, 1813. From the rooms of the Chicago Historical Society, we obtain the following interesting facts in his genealogy, extending back to the seventh generation, and beginning with the first representative of the family in America:

First Generation. Mr. William Douglas, of Boston, Massachusetts, A. D. 1640. Married Ann, daughter of Thomas Mable, of Kingstead, Northamptonshire, England. The birth of their son William is recorded at Boston, as the "1 (2) 1645," i. e. March 1, 1645. The family afterwards removed and settled at New London, Conn., where Mr. William Douglas was one of the leading men of the colony, deacon of the church, representative in the colonial legislature in 1672, and during King Philip's Indian War was appointed commissary of the army. The following, from Gov. Bradstreet's journal, gives the date of his death: "1682, July 26th, Mr. William Douglas, one of ye deacons of this church, died in ye 72d year of his age. He was an able Christian, and this poor church will much miss him."

Second Generation. His son, William Douglas, born as above, married, December 18th, 1667, Abiah Hough, daughter of Mr. William Hough, of New London, Conn., (who was a son of Edward Hough, of West Chester, Cheshire, England,) by whom he had two sons and five daughters.

Third Generation. Of these sons the oldest, William Douglas, was born April 19th, 1672, and removed to Plainfield, Conn., where he was a deacon in the church. By his wife, Sarah, he had eight sons and three daughters.

Fourth Generation. The youngest of these children was Asa Douglas, born Dec. 11th, 1715. Asa Douglas, by his wife Rebecca, had seven sons and six daughters. He died Nov. 12th, 1792.

Fifth Generation. The twelfth child of Asa and Rebecca Douglas was Benajah Douglas, born May 10th, 1762. He married Patty Arnold, daughter of Stephen Arnold, Esq.

(3)

Sixth Generation. The father of our late Senator was Stephen Arnold **Douglas**, son of Benajah and Patty Douglas, as above. He was born in the State of New York, and was a physician of considerable repute. He died suddenly of apoplexy, in 1813, when his son (Stephen Arnold) was only two months old.

It appears from this interesting recital that Senator Douglas came of distinguished Puritan stock. The indomitable energy of his character, and the iron will which made him always a master of circumstances, mark him a lineal descendant of the Mayflower.

Brought up on a farm under his mother's care, **and receiving a** common school education, he desired, at the age **of fifteen, to pre**pare for **college. His** family being unable to defray the **expense,** he left **the farm** and apprenticed himself to **a cabinet maker at** Middlebury, where he labored a year and a half. He then entered an academy at Brandon, where he studied another year. **His mother** having married Mr. Granger of Ontario Co., N. Y., Stephen removed with her to Canandaigua where he entered another academy. He remained at Canandaigua two years and a half, studying law at the same time that he acquired his academical education. **In the spring of 1833, he** came west to find an eligible place to practice law, going successively to Cleveland, Cincinnati, Louisville, St. Louis and Jacksonville, Ill. At Jacksonville he found himself reduced to his last shilling, and went on foot to Winchester (Scott county) to get employment as a school teacher, taking with him a few law books with which to perfect himself in his chosen profession. Obtaining six dollars for three days' work as **clerk** to an auctioneer **he hired a** room and opened a school, teaching by day, studying by night and practicing before justices of the peace on Saturday afternoons. **In March, 1834, he opened an** office for law business, and was so successful that before the expiration of the year, he was chosen Attorney General of the **state by the** Legislature. He resigned the office shortly afterwards and was elected a member of the Legislature from Morgan county. His rise from that time to the present was brilliant **and rapid,** and, until betrayed by the Southern leaders for whom he had done so much, marked by hardly a single **defeat.**

In **1837 he was** appointed **by President Van Buren** register of the land office at Springfield. **In the same year he** received the Democratic nomination for Congress in a **district embracing the whole northern** part of the **State. His** competitor was John T. Stuart, Esq., of Springfield. Something over 36,000 votes were cast, and **Mr.** Stuart was **declared** elected by a majority of *five.* Neither Mr. Douglas nor Mr. Stuart nor **any** one else have ever **been able to say which candidate** actually received the majority,

BIRTHPLACE OF SENATOR DOUGLAS, AT BRANDON, VT.

but it is certain that Mr. Stuart obtained the seat. In 1840 Mr. Douglas was appointed Secretary of State. In 1841 he was chosen by the legislature a judge of the Supreme Court. In 1843 he was nominated for Congress, and was elected by 400 majority in a Whig district. He was re-elected in 1844 by 1,900 majority, and again in 1846 by 3,000 majority. The same year he was chosen by the legislature to a seat in the United States Senate, which he took on the 4th of March, 1847, and has occupied without interruption ever since. His present term would have expired March 4th, 1865.

Mr. Douglas' career in Congress is familiar to almost every citizen of Illinois. Hardly a measure of national moment has been before that body during the past seventeen years without receiving the imprint of his strong and comprehensive intellect. The Oregon bill, the Jackson resolutions, the admission, respectively, of Florida, Iowa, Wisconsin, Minnesota and California; the maritime laws of the great lakes and rivers of the West; the war with Mexico; the compromise measures of 1850; the Kansas and Nebraska Act; the Pacific Railroad bills; the Clayton-Bulwer treaty, and the Lecompton Constitution, all bear the marks of his energy and ability in a greater degree than of any other contemporary statesman. In the Democratic National Convention of 1852, Mr. Douglas received 92 votes for the Presidential nomination, and in the Convention of 1856 he received 121. We need hardly recur to the conventions of Charleston and Baltimore last year, where the delegates from the North clung to him with the energy of desperation, and where the South deliberately broke the party in twain for the purpose of defeating the only candidate who could have been elected, and thus affording themselves a pretext for destroying the Union. It is little enough to say, in concluding this biographical sketch, that for the past four years at least the Democratic party has *existed* in and by Stephen A. Douglas. Neither Jackson nor Van Buren, in their palmiest days, ever reigned with more perfect and unquestioned sway than he in the great political division to which he belonged.

Mr. Douglas was married April 7, 1847, to Miss Martha D. Martin, of Rockingham county, N. C., by whom he had three children, two of whom are living. She died Jan. 19, 1853. He was again married Nov. 20, 1856, to Miss Adele Cutts, daughter of James Madison Cutts, Esq., second comptroller of the Treasury, by whom he had a daughter, who died about a year and a half ago.

It is well known that the Chicago *Tribune* has had no sympathy with the political movements of the late Senator since 1853. He was content to go his way, and we ours. He had one line of policy, and we another. In all these years of difference, we have shared with others the animosity that our prejudices or his acts provoked; and he even was not exempt from the infirmity which afflicts all partisans. We draw a veil over that distracted period, and leave the historian to decide whether he and his friends, or his opposers, ourselves among the number, were right. We have nothing to apologize for—nothing to extenuate—and he would have had nothing to unsay had he lived. But in all partisan strifes there come moments when the enmities and hates engendered by conflicting views and personal ambitions, are beaten down and conquered by danger which all men must share. One of these moments has been upon us; it brought about a union which years would have cemented. Only yesterday Judge Douglass and the *Tribune* stood upon the same platform. The imminent peril of the present had put all old things out of sight; and side by side with him we stood for the defense, the honor and the perpetuity of the great Republic; and now uncovered and reverently looking into his grave, we can say that a Patriot reposes therein. In revolutions, the events of a day are equal to the work which years of peace accomplish. The rude shock of arms lately encountered, awakened him to the true designs of the men with whom he had acted; and the same potent cause revealed him to us in an aspect as unwonted as it was glorious. If he had been mistaken in those for whom he had hazarded so much, we were not less so in him whom we so earnestly opposed. If he found them treacherous and false, the country saw him noble and true. Under all that seemed to contemporaries of the opposite school, selfish, ambitious and unpatriotic, was felt to be that enduring basis out of which devotion and patriotism grow. To-day, the signs of sorrow and the habiliments of woe, the subdued voice, the measured tread and the look of grief every where observable among all parties and men of all creeds, are proofs that the heart of the country is wounded, and the people, now all sensible of his value, will profoundly and sincerely mourn their irreparable loss.

In his last days, he gave those who stood near to minister to his wants, the most convincing assurances of the depth and earnestness of the lively love of country that filled his heart. In his waking hours, as well as in those moments when the violence of his disease unseated his great intellect, he was busy with national events, and the conflict that is now upon us. It was his last wish that the work which will regenerate the country while rescuing it from his enemies, should go rapidly on. To one, in a wandering moment, he said, "I station you at the Relay House. Move on!" Of another he asked, "Why do we stand still? let us press on! Let us to Alexandria quick!" To still another he said, "Telegraph to the President, and let the column move on!" And so, throughout the progress of the disease, which struck him down— he was thinking of his country and her peril. At Washington, in his imaginings, and in the command for which nature had fitted him, and which would have been bestowed had he lived, he seemed to direct events and dictate victory. And when the lucid intervals came, he was, if not so emphatic, not less sincere. The salvation of the Republic was uppermost in his thoughts by day and by night. His own condition, the imminent peril of death, his complicated affairs, gave him no concern. Almost his last coherent words were an ardent wish for the honor and prosperity of the Republic, by the defeat and dispersion of her enemies. The country, regardless of party distinctions, wherever the love of the stars and stripes is not repressed by the terrorism which he knew and hated, will treasure up his dying prayer and make his hopes and aspirations the rule of patriotic endeavor.

We need say nothing of the personal characteristics of Stephen A. Douglas. There is no cabin in America to which his name has not gone. There is no man, however humble or unfit, who from the praise of his friends, often indiscreet, or the abuse of his enemies, more frequently undeserved, has not made up an estimate of the man. He was undeniably great. He had a great brain, in which size did not repress activity. He had a will which was as inflexible as iron. He had a courage which bordered at times upon audacity. He had great affections, and by consequence great passions—he could hate as well as love. He had great vigor of constitution, and, all men said, a firm hold upon the strings of life. He had the power of drawing men to him with the grasp and vigor of a giant. No one since Henry Clay has had such hosts of friends who would do his will or die in the attempt. He had great ambition, which he sought to gratify by great events. Hence he was an orator and politician; and as both he greatly excelled. Nature fitted him to make a mark in the world; and he could not have been placed where he would not have graven his name. He has gone from us at a moment when his loss will most be felt. In the vigor of early manhood, without having yet attained the full maturity of his powers as an orator or thinker; but of ripened experience and broad culture, he has fallen. Another decade, when the voice of war is forgotten, would have witnessed the gratification of the object of his later strifes. His country at peace in all its parts and with all the world, the arrogant slave power humiliated partly by his **courageous efforts,** would have seen his elevation to the **position that he** would have filled with conspicuous ability. That was among the readable certainties of the future. But he has gone. The good and evil of his life remain, for the instruction of those who will do the work from which he is dissevered forever. Let us who are left, emulous of that fervid love of country which will make his name glorious, press on in the direction in which, when living, his face was set. His last public speech is the standard by which his life is to be measured. We remember him by **that,** and lay down therefor this tribute of gratitude and praise.

SENATOR DOUGLAS died on the 3d of June, 1861, at the Tremont House, in the city of Chicago, about four weeks after his **great** speech before the State Legislature, and his last public **address in the old "** Wigwam," on Market street, where **Abraham Lincoln was nominated, one** year before, for President.

His death was pronounced by his physicians **to be** the result **of fever of** a typhoid nature, brought on by extreme mental and physical labor during the few last years of his life, together with the excitement and anxiety caused by the precarious condition of the country upon the eve of a great civil war. There was probably not a man **in** all the land who possessed a keener sense of the disastrous and doubtful consequences of such a revolution as was about to burst forth, than Senator Douglas.

His remains were embalmed, and for some time lay "in state" at **Bryan** Hall. An immense concourse of people, irre**spective** of political or religious differences, viewed the mortal **remains with** loving and respectful deference.

The body was then borne to the place whereon he had intended to **build** his homestead, and there, buried underneath the track of a primitive highway, once a stage road leading from the east along the lake shore to Chicago, and within a few feet of a great railway of which he was the chief promoter and father, he "sleeps his last sleep" within sound of the beating waves of Lake Michigan and of the rushing trains.

The funeral procession extended half-way from the City Hall to the grave, and all parties and creeds vied with each other to honor the dead Senator. He was buried with Masonic ceremonies, and the Roman Catholic bishop of the diocese accorded such honors as he could under the laws of his church.

A space, sixteen feet square, was immediately inclosed by a rude board fence, and in two weeks this inclosure presented a level spot of sand, without a shrub or spear of grass to greet the visitor to this then lonely place.

Steps were soon taken, however, to beautify and protect the grave.

[From Chicago Tribune, July 24, 1861.]
THE RESTING PLACE OF DOUGLAS.

An unusual degree of interest is manifest among our citizens, in the direction of suitable improvement and adornment of the last resting place of Douglas at Cottage Grove. The following we find in the *Post* of yesterday, alluding to the same:

"The rough fence boards were inscribed all over with the names of visitors, representing nearly every section of the Union that is still loyal to the constitution. Here are a few of them:"

And then our contemporary gives a list of these scribblers, who would have been quite as likely to have scrawled their autographs on the memorial marble itself. It is a lamentable American weakness, the cheapest kind of "Brummagem" vanity, that incites these scrawling tribes to the scoring of their address on every place of public resort, whether cemetery or public building, no matter how sacred or how costly. For ourselves we desire to see the last resting place of the illustrious dead at Cottage Grove marked appropriately, as it will be, by a tribute worthy the fame of the sleeper that rests beneath. We shall hope to see it adorned with rich and permanent memorials, and a resort of all visitors to our city. We are glad to learn that our talented young fellow citizen, **Leo. W. Volk** has already been put in charge of the preparation of some plan of such adornment. Let it be handsome, liberal, proper. But then will the scrawlers and scribblers of their own ill-written names, spare the place their profanation. Visitors who pause to read the name of "Douglas," cut in marble or enduring bronze, will be little edified to learn, from handwriting hard by, that "Peter Smith" lives in Porkopolis, or "Mary Snooks" in Hedgepole.

The "Invincible Club" interested itself, and the City Council of Chicago made its first and only appropriation of fifty dollars in behalf of a new fence.

Some flowers from Lake View and evergreens from Egandale were donated by friends, and with volunteer work from neighbors in the vicinity, the inclosure was soon made to look quite neat and respectable.

While this tribute of love and respect was being performed, and the green sod laid over and around the grave, there came like a thunder-clap the announcement of the disastrous battle of Manassas, or Bull Run. How dark indeed was this day!

In the following September, the writer was authorized by Mrs. Douglas to take charge as custodian of the grave and the estate at Cottage Grove. A short time previous he received from her the following letter:

Mr. Leonard W. Volk:

"*My Dear Sir:*—I have not words to tell you how thankful I am; and your young friends have undertaken a task which will I well know, be to you each one a labor of love. The lonely and deserted appearance of that cherished grave has never left my memory since I last saw it for one moment. I was anxious to make some better arrangement before I left Chicago, but my grief made me too helpless to carry out my intention, and friends advised me to leave it to them. Any plan your taste may suggest will be agreeable to me. With renewed thanks,

I am yours,
                    Adele Douglas.

Washington, July 25th, 1861."

FIRST CALL FOR A MEETING.

CHICAGO, October 19th, 1861.

Sir: A meeting of gentlemen interested in providing an efficient organization for the erection of a suitable monument in honor of the late Hon. STEPHEN A. DOUGLAS, and as a grateful recognition of the illustrious services rendered by him to his country, will be held at the parlor of the Tremont House, on Tuesday, October 22, 1861, at 8 o'clock, P. M.

You are respectfully requested to be present and participate in the proposed meeting.

Respectfully,
Your obedient servants,
J. W. SHEAHAN,
S. W. FULLER,
S. H. KERFOOT,
W. C. GOUDY,
THOMAS DRUMMOND,
DAVID A. GAGE,
J. P. CLARKSON,
LEONARD W. VOLK.

[From a Morning Paper.]

A meeting of citizens was held at the Tremont house last evening, for the inauguration of the popular movement towards the erection of a monument to the memory of Stephen A. Douglas. There was a full attendance of influential and respectable citizens, and the matter was discussed at considerable length. The sentiment of the meeting was in favor of making the movement a popular one by appealing to every class of citizens. To effect this, it was deemed advisable that the subscription should be limited to one dollar for each person,—a sum which every friend of the great statesman and his doctrines will give with cheerful readiness.

It is proposed to erect a monument which shall cost one hundred or one hundred and fifty thousand dollars. This sum will furnish a work of art which will be a worthy token of the regard in which the great statesman was held by the nation; and will constitute an enduring ornament among the institutions of the city of Chicago. No plans have yet been presented, but the best talent in the country will be employed on the designs, and the monument will be of magnificent and tasteful proportions.

A committee was apppointed to deliberate on the best **method of** carrying out the design of the meeting, who will report at a future session. **This committee** consisted **of** the following gentlemen, viz: Hon. John M. Wilson, L. W. **Volk, W.** C. Goudy, H. G. Miller, S. W. Fuller, J. W. Sheahan, J. M. Rountree.

ORGANIZATION OF THE MONUMENT ASSOCIATION.

[From Chicago Times, Nov. 9, 1861.]

An adjourned meeting **of** citizens to take into consideration **the erection of a** monument to **the** memory of Stephen A. Douglas, **was held** last evening at the Tremont House. The meeting was organized by the election of Judge Scates **as chairman,** and W. C. **Goudy** as secretary.

H. G. Miller, from a committee appointed **at a previous** meeting, **to** propose a plan for carrying out the object **in** view, reported in **favor** of founding an incorporated company **under an** act of the Legislature entitled, "An act for the Incorporation of Benevolent, **Educational,** Literary, **Musical, Scientific and** Missionary Societies, including Societies **Formed for** Mutual Improvement, or for the **Promotion of** the Arts," approved February **24,** 1859, the incorporated company to be named "The Douglas Monument Association," **and** its object to be the erection of a monument to the memory of the late Stephen Arnold Douglas, with a capital stock of one hundred and fifty thousand dollars, divided into one hundred and **fifty** thousand shares, of one dollar each. The operations of the association are to be carried on in the city of Chicago.

The committee **were** in favor of effecting a permanent organization by special act of the Legislature.

Pro**fes**sor McChesney, in behalf of a committee of **the board of trustees of** the University of Chicago, stated that the board had **resolved** that the **centre** building of the University, including the tower, should be called **Douglas** Hall, and that they desired that the name should be inscribed upon a tablet and embodied therein, **and that the remains of Judge Douglas** be placed in the tower. He thought that the propriety and fitness of this action was apparent from **the relation** of Judge Douglas to the University, he having taken a zealous interest in the establishment of that institution, and donated **to it** nearly one hundred thousand dollars. He thought that such a tower as was proposed would be the most fit and appropriate monument that could be erected. The board had already made an appeal for means to carry out this plan.

L. W. Volk presented a plan of organization of **an association, the affairs** of which should be managed by a **board of eighteen trustees,** and memberships to which should be secured by the contribution of one dollar.

The various plans were discussed at some length. Judge Scates was of the opinion that the monument should be erected independently of the University. Many would wish to contribute to the one who would not be willing to give aid to the other. He thought the object could be more quickly and surely accomplished by having the one distinct object in view, and urged that some definite organization be effected as soon as practicable.

The report of the committee was laid on the table.

The plan of Mr. Volk was then adopted.

The organization is as follows:

Article First.—This association shall be known as the "DOUGLAS MONUMENT ASSOCIATION."

Article Second.—All persons contributing not less than the sum of one dollar to its object shall be considered members of the Association, and be entitled to a diploma or certificate of membership.

Article Third.—For the energetic and successful prosecution of the object of this Association, namely, the erection of a suitable monument in honor of the late Hon. Stephen Arnold Douglas, to be placed over his remains at Cottage Grove, or elsewhere near Chicago—a Board of Trustees, to consist of eighteen persons, a majority of whom, at least, shall be residents of Chicago, or within a distance therefrom convenient for attendance at its meetings, shall be forthwith appointed, this association to select twelve members, and the residue to be elected hereafter by said twelve members so selected; to which said Board shall be committed:

1. All the active, executive and legal powers of the Association without reserve, and especially the entire charge of selecting and deciding upon a plan for said monument.

2. The adoption of such plan or plans for the raising and collection of contributions in aid of its construction and completion as they shall judge advisable.

3. The contracting with such party or parties for the complete construction of the proposed monument, at such time, and within such conditions as they may approve.

Article Fourth.—1. Said board shall be known as the "Board of Trustees of the Douglas Monument Association."

2. The whole number of said board shall be divided into three equal sections, one section to retire alternately every five years; and all vacancies in the board made by such retirement, by resignation, disability, death, or otherwise, to be filled by the remaining members.

3. Said board shall organize by the election, at such times as they may direct, of a president, treasurer, and secretary (which secretary, at their discretion, may be outside of their body, to be of approved capacity, integrity, and particular abilities for the office, and receive, at their discretion, a remuneration for his services), as also of an executive committee of the board for the better transaction of its business,—together with such other officers or agents as they may judge needful and proper.

4. Said board shall make and establish such rules and regulations relating to its meetings and organization, the duties of its officers and agents, and the transaction of its business, as in their judgment shall be thought best.

5. Said board shall hold, through its treasurer, all property or moneys now or hereafter to be acquired in the name or for the purposes of this Association; shall have a legal seal, and shall seasonably secure such legal incorporation, under the authority of the Legislature or of existing laws, as shall give full validity to its acts.

6. Said board shall hold themselves individually, and exclusively of the Association, responsible for all expenditures of money made by them beyond such amounts as are or have been actually collected and paid in to their treasurer.

7. Said board may, at their discretion, elect individuals of this or any other State to be honorary members thereof, or of the Association in general, under such provisions or conditions as they may see fit to establish; *provided*, that no person, upon the condition of pecuniary contribution, shall be made an honorary member of the Association upon the payment of a sum less than twenty dollars; nor an honorary member of the board of trustees upon the payment of a sum less than one hundred dollars.

8. Said board shall take seasonable steps to secure, as a preliminary to, and on the condition precedent of, the completion of the proposed monument, the guaranty of the fee of the land or such part thereof as may be required for the suitable arrangement of

said monument, or otherwise provide for the perpetual and undisturbed security of the same.

9. Upon the full completion of said monument, it shall be the duty of said board to have set apart and provided a sufficient permanent fund, to be put at interest, the annual proceeds of which shall be applied for the preservation, care, and repair of said monument and land, or, at their election, to convey to the city of Chicago, or the state of Illinois, said monument or land, or both, upon the guaranty of the authorities so receiving the same, that said monument and the land upon which it stands shall be perpetually kept in due preservation and care for all time.

Article Fifth.—It is the intention of this association to intrust said board with as full and complete powers as may be necessary for the execution of the trust hereby committed to them, whether the same are herein expressed or not.

Article Sixth.—Said board shall, as often as once in each year, publish a full account of their proceedings, as also of their receipts and expenditures, in behalf of said monument, duly certified; for the information of the members of this association and the public.

The meeting then adjourned, subject to the call of a committee of three.

The following are the names of the subscribers to the foregoing Articles of Association, arranged as originally signed, which were obtained by Mr. Volk, all of whom paid one dollar:

WALTER B. SCATES,	WM. C. GOUDY,
LEONARD W. VOLK,	J. P. CLARKSON,
SAML. W. FULLER,	E. B. McCAGG,
S. H. KERFOOT,	J. L. MARSH,
THOS. B. BRYAN,	E. VAN BUREN,
JNO. G. ROGERS,	GEO. A. MEECH,
PHILIP CO. LEY,	M. B. THOMAS,
J. W. FOSTER,	EDWIN H. SHELDON,
JAMES ROBB,	J. H. ROBERTS,
W. B. OGDEN,	M. W FULLER,
C. R. STARKWEATHER,	HENRY G. MILLER,
WILLIAM BARRY,	JOHN V. EUSTACE,
JOHN TYRRELL,	JOHN M. ROUNTREE,
W. K. McALLISTER,	J. H. HUBBARD,
OBEDIAH JACKSON, Jr.,	T. S. FITCH,
D. CAMERON, Jr.,	JOHN N. JEWETT,
AARON HAVEN,	B. S. MORRIS,
J. H. McCHESNEY,	WM. H. BRADLEY,
D. A. GAGE,	WM. H. KING,
W. F. STOREY,	IRA SCOTT,
H. A. TUCKER,	J. M. PARKER,
GEO. P. A. HEALY,	U. F. LINDER,
THOMAS DRUMMOND,	J. C. BURROUGHS,

C. H. McCORMICK,	GEO. S. KIMBERLY,
EDWIN BURNHAM,	B. G. CAULFIELD,
C. R. BURNHAM,	JOHN M. WILSON,
E. HEMPSTEAD,	EDW. I. TINKHAM,
SOL. A. SMITH,	R. A. B. MILLS,
S. S. HAYES,	H. O. STONE,
JOS. KNOX,	J. H. DUNHAM,
J. Q. HOYT,	F. A. BRYAN,
C. WATROUS,	**JOHN PARMLY**,
H. D. COLVIN,	E. C. ROGERS,
GEO. M. GRADY,	MARTIN RYERSON,
A. T KING,	MALCOLM McDONALD,
JAMES LARMON,	JOHN COMISKEY,
P. A. HOYNE,	B. McVICKAR,
ANDRE MATTESON,	F. C. SHERMAN,
A. M. HERRINGTON,	HENRY FULLER,
WIRT DEXTER,	GEO. W. FULLER,
R. T. MERRICK,	J. H WOODWORTH,
M. PARKER,	W. W. WAITE,
JOHN GARRICK,	C. R JONES,
HORACE A. HURLBUT,	FRANK PARMELEE,
G. S. HUBBARD,	JOHN B. TURNER,
F. A. EASTMAN,	V. C. TURNER,
J. M. DOUGLAS,	J. W CONNETT,
C. WALSH,	J. B. OLCOTT,
JAS. GRANT WILSON,	L. D. LANGLY,
R. B. MASON,	JULIAN S. RUMSEY,
W. L. NEWBERRY,	**R. R BALL**,
W. G. SHERMAN,	**S. B. GOOKINS**,
JOHN VAN ARMAN,	**J. M. WALKER**.

MEETING OF THE DOUGLAS MONUMENT ASSOCIATION.

A MEETING of the members of the Douglas Monument Association was held at the Tremont House, December 5, 1861, in pursuance of the call of the committee appointed for that purpose, to select twelve trustees of the Douglas Monument Association, which was called to order by W. C. Goudy, Esq.

On motion, Hon. S. W. Fuller was elected **Chairman** and **W. C. Goudy** Secretary.

On motion of Aaron **Haven, Esq., a committee of** five was appointed, consisting of **Aaron** Haven, **Wm. Barry, H.** G. Miller, L. **W. Volk**, and B. G. Caulfield, to nominate twelve persons for the office of **trustees.**

The committee retired **and** reported the names of the following **persons** for the office of trustees, to-wit: John **B.** Turner, John D. **Caton,** Wm. B. Ogden, Walter B. Scates, Wm. Barry, Sam'l W. Fuller, John M. Douglas, Wm. C. Goudy, David A. Gage, John S. Newhouse, Francis C. Sherman, and Thos. **B.** Bryan.

Hon. S. B. Gookins moved that the report be adopted, and the persons nominated be elected, which motion was carried unanimously.

Rev. Wm. Barry moved that John B. Turner, Esq., be requested to call the first meeting of the Board of Trustees, and that the secretary notify the persons elected trustees, of their selection.

On motion the meeting adjourned.

S. W. FULLER, Chairman.
W. C. GOUDY, Secretary.

On the 19th of October, 1861, was issued a call, signed by a number of well-known citizens, requesting a meeting of the friends of the late Senator Douglas, for the purpose of devising the most judicious plan of organization to carry out the wish of his friends and admirers for the erection of a suitable monument over his remains.

Pursuant to the call, the meeting was numerously attended, and a marked interest and enthusiasm were manifested in the proposed object.

At a subsequent meeting, held on the 8th of November, articles of association were adopted, to form the proposed constitution, and a committee was appointed to procure signatures to the same, and to call a full meeting of the subscribers, who were to select, in accordance with the constitution, twelve trustees, to whom the interests and business of the association were to be committed.

After more than one hundred names had been obtained by the committee, the meeting was called, at which twelve gentlemen were unanimously chosen by the association as its trustees, who, at subsequent meetings of their body, filled up their number to eighteen by the selection of six others, and elected their officers and executive committee, in compliance with the constitution. They also adopted a code of by-laws for their own regulation, together with an appeal to the public in behalf of their patriotic object.

BOARD OF TRUSTEES.

Hon. John B. Turner, Chicago; General William A. Richardson, Quincy; Hon. John D. Caton, Ottawa; Hon. William B. Ogden, Chicago; Hon. Walter B. Scates, Chicago; Rt. Rev. James Duggan, D. D., Chicago; Rev. William Barry, Chicago; Hon. James C. Allen, Palestine; Hon. Samuel H. Treat, Springfield; Hon. William C. Goudy, Chicago; Thomas B. Bryan, Esq., Chicago; David A. Gage, Esq., Chicago; Hon. Francis C. Sherman, Chicago; Hon.

Samuel W. Fuller, Chicago; Col. John Dement, Dixon; Col. John A. Logan, Benton; **John** M. Douglas, Esq., Chicago; John S. Newhouse, Esq., Chicago.

OFFICERS.

Walter B. Scates, President; Thomas B. Bryan, 1st Vice President; William C. Goudy, 2d Vice President; David **A. Gage**, Treasurer; Leonard W. Volk, Secretary.

EXECUTIVE COMMITTEE.

Walter B. Scates, President; Rt. Rev. Bishop Duggan, **John B.** Turner, Francis C. Sherman, David A. **Gage**, Treasurer; **Leonard** W. Volk, Secretary.

THE DOUGLAS MONUMENT ASSOCIATION.

APPEAL TO THE PEOPLE.

THE Board of Trustees, appointed by the Douglas Monument Association, being duly organized for the execution of the patriotic enterprise entrusted to their charge, respectfully submit their doings and design to the public, confident that no urgent appeal is needed to the friends of the late Stephen A. Douglas to assist in the proposed tribute of honor and gratitude to that illustrious statesman and patriot. Born among the free hills of New England, his early life passed in New York, his maturer years consecrated with generous and never-faltering devotion to his country, he has long been known as the distinguished representative of the West in the councils of the nation, whose boldness, courage, enthusiasm, and brilliant talents elevated him to an almost unrivalled power and commanding influence among his countrymen—equal for every emergency, daunted by no obstacle, and acquiring new greatness even in disaster and seeming defeat; giving him an acknowledged place in the constellation of eminent statesmen and patriots whose names will ever illumine the history of our country.

Without recalling the various and eventful occasions of his brilliant career as a politician and statesman, in which he won the renown which was so willingly and warmly conceded to him, it needs only to recur to his last appeals of a true and magnanimous patriotism in behalf of his imperiled country, rallying all hearts to a loyal and self-sacrificing maintenance of the Union of these States, and the Constitution of our hitherto great and united Republic, to vindicate his full claim to an honorary and grateful remembrance, now that he has fallen in the meridian of his fame, when, never more than now, his eloquent voice and inspiring courage are needed in his country's hour of darkness and trial.

In the tranquil rest of the grave the departed can be reached indeed by no honors a grateful country can rear over his remains. But not less to ourselves and to our country, and to the generations yet unborn who are to enter upon the sacred heritage and responsibilities of freemen, than to him is it due, that his grave should not be unmarked by some enduring tribute of national honors and gratitude.

In seeking to secure a fitting monument to perpetuate the name of DOUGLAS, the trustees feel assured that they but represent the warm and unanimous sentiment which found prompt utterance throughout our country on his lamented death; and they desire to be actuated in the accomplishment of the sacred charge committed to them by an inviolable trust to what is due alike to the honored dead, and to the sentiments which consecrate his memory in the hearts of his friends and countrymen.

In submitting the plan of organization and proceedings adopted for and by this board, it is hoped that the same will commend itself to the general confidence and approval.

It is believed that the judicious precautions early adopted will be a sufficient guarantee that all due care, fidelity and good judgment will be employed to secure an early and satisfactory achievement of the work they have undertaken. The trustees presume to make no demands, nor do they prescribe limits in their appeal to Mr. Douglas' friends. They forbear at this time even from presenting any anticipatory design for the proposed monument, either in respect to its form or cost, beyond such suggestions as propriety may dictate, leaving the matter finally to be determined hereafter by what shall appear to be the wish of the public, as expressed in their voluntary benefactions to his memory. It has been the desire of this board to afford the broadest scope to the liberality of the public, and to do this in such a manner as to connect the names of the humblest contributors with the association formed to honor the departed statesman. The trustees cannot hope, without the concurring vigilance of the public, to guard against all contingencies of imposture or misplaced confidence in the collections proposed by them. They beg to have it distinctly understood that all authorized agents of this board will carry with them authentic credentials under the seal of the association, which, it is hoped, may guard with due caution against misrepresentation and fraud.

In prosecuting their proposed collections, it is the intention of the board to afford opportunity to the friends of the late Mr. Douglas in all parts of the country to unite in this national tribute to his memory. To this end they would be gladly assisted by the voluntary organization of local auxiliary associations, to be under judicious and reliable management, with which this board may be in communication, and to which diplomas will be forwarded in return for such moneys as are collected and forwarded.

Should any individuals feel prompted to anticipate a direct appeal by a voluntary transmission of money in aid of the object, the same can be forwarded by mail, or otherwise, to the treasurer. The appeal which this board makes to the fellow countrymen and friends of the late Mr. Douglas cannot be deemed untimely, even amidst the dark hour of the republic, and the privations and distress of an unnatural war. None more than that patriotic statesman sought to avert, by just and constitutional aims, legitimate complaint; none more than he, when treason menaced the foundations of our national existence, and glory proclaimed in truer and more inspiring tones, his steadfast loyalty and everlasting fidelity to the Union and Constitution, bequeathing to his country in his dying words unquestioned tokens of the allegiance which had inspired his whole life, and which, breathing from his silent grave, may yet reanimate and restore the divided glory of our common country.

Surely it is not untimely to rear now enduring marble over his honored remains, bearing forever the last words which burst from his dying lips, "TELL MY CHILDREN TO OBEY THE LAWS, AND UPHOLD THE CONSTITUTION."

A constitution and code of by-laws were duly adopted by the trustees, for the government of the association, and the constitution provided that the secretary should receive as compensation for his services the sum of one thousand dollars per annum. No other officer or trustee was to receive compensation for any service rendered.

The following was drafted by Mr. Goudy, and presented to the Legislature and passed:

AN ACT TO INCORPORATE THE DOUGLAS MONUMENT ASSOCIATION.

SEC. 1. Be it enacted by the people of the State of Illinois, represented in the general assembly, That William A. Richardson, Francis C. Sherman, William B. Ogden, John B. Turner, James Duggan, Samuel H. Treat, William C. Goudy, John D. Caton, Walter B. Scates, Thomas B. Bryan, William Barry, Samuel W Fuller, Samuel S. Marshall, James C. Allen, John Dement, John M. Douglas, David A. Gage and John S. Newhouse, and their successors, be and are hereby created a corporate body, under the name and style of "The Douglas Monument Association," and by that name may sue and be sued, shall have a seal, and exercise all the powers necessary to carry out and effect the purposes of the act.

SEC. 2. The said corporators shall constitute the first board of trustees of the Douglas Monument Association; and their division into three equal sections (each section to retire alternately every five years), heretofore made by the preliminary organization of said association, is hereby ratified and confirmed; and all vacancies in the board made by such retirement, resignation, disability, death or otherwise, shall be filled by the remaining members of said board.

SEC. 3. All persons contributing not less than the sum of one dollar to its objects, shall be considered members of the association, and be entitled to a diploma or certificate of membership.

SEC. 4. The said corporation is created for the purpose of erecting a suitable monument in honor of the late Stephen A. Douglas, to be placed over or near his remains, at Cottage Grove, near the city of Chicago; and shall have power to select and decide upon a plan for said monument; to adopt plans for raising and collecting contributions in aid of its construction and completion; and to contract for the construction of the proposed monument.

SEC. 5. The said board of trustees may organize by the election of a president, vice-president, secretary (who may be outside their body), treasurer, and also an executive committee, together with such other officers or agents as they may deem proper; and they may make and establish such rules and regulations relating to its meetings and organization, the duties of its officers and agents, and the transaction of its business, as in their judgment shall be thought best.

SEC. 6. The said corporation shall have power to hold such real estate, whether acquired by purchase, gift or devise, as may be necessary for the purpose of effecting the purposes hereinbefore mentioned, and also have power to take, receive or hold real estate or personal effects, that may be granted, devised, bequeathed or donated to said corporation, and to sell and convey the same for the purpose of aiding the erection and care of said monument or improving the grounds belonging thereto.

SEC. 7. The board of trustees shall publish a full account of their proceedings, and of their receipts and expenditures in behalf of said monument, duly certified, as often as once in each year, for the information of the members of the association and the public.

SEC. 8. The proceedings and organization of the Douglas Monument Association had under articles of association adopted on the 8th day of November, 1861, are hereby confirmed, and shall be treated with like effect as if made by the corporation now created by this act.

SEC. 9. This act shall take effect and be in force from and after its passage.

Approved February 11, 1863.

The work of collecting funds to carry forward the object was now the order. A temporary place of meeting for the trustees was obtained, and some cheap office furniture and stationery purchased. Also an engraving on steel for diplomas of membership and printing of pamphlets and circulars were ordered, special agents were appointed to canvass for subscriptions, and local agencies established in different places. But the great Rebellion absorbed all interests. "Camp Douglas," adjacent to the grave of the namesake, with its first installment of Confederate prisoners of war from Fort Donelson, and the thousands of Union soldiers, to the end of the conflict attracted more attention than the humble grave of Douglas. The almost universal answer to appeals for money to build the proposed monument, was, "Wait till the war is over; the government must have aid, and the sick, wounded and dying soldiers must first be cared for; and if the cause of the Union fails, then no monuments need be erected to Douglas or any other statesman." Who could press for subscriptions after such answers? Yet, in the face of all these difficulties, it was pressed and never lost sight of.

New men—statesmen, patriots and heroes came upon the stage and went off in rapid succession, completely overshadowing for a time those great men who died before the struggle began. In a brief time contributions were being solicited not only for the relief of the sick and wounded soldiers, but for the dead soldiers' monuments.

The agents of the association soon threw up their commissions, as most of them were not able to collect sufficient to pay their expenses.

The authorities of the University of Chicago had their agents, Gen. U. F. Linder and others, in the field canvassing and lecturing for funds for the "Douglas monument" (meaning the tower of that institution) some months before the monument association got organized and at work.

This action on the part of the University proved a serious drawback on the outstart, as it was difficult to make people unstand amid the turmoil and prevailing excitement, which object was the proper one to contribute to, and probably some contributions to agents were made and applied contrary to the donors' intentions. During this "dark age" of the war, the writer sustained great difficulty in keeping the grounds in which the grave of Douglas was located free from hospital and general camp purposes. The grave was infested by all manner of trespassers and desecrators, such as usually hover about military camps.

For some time after the association organized, the meetings of the trustees were regularly attended, but owing to the public attention being so completely absorbed in the daily and exciting events of the war, and after its close it was difficult to obtain quorums for the transaction of business.

In 1863, during the absence of President Walter B. Scates in the army, the following circular was addressed to the members of the State Legislature:

CHICAGO, May 22, 1863.

Sir:—The undersigned, members of the executive committee of the trustees of The Douglas Monument Association, desire to make a brief statement of their labors, and to respectfully ask your efficient aid and co-operation in the furtherance of their patriotic endeavors to rear, in behalf of the people, a befitting monument over the remains of the late STEPHEN A. DOUGLAS.

It is now two years since his lamented death, and yet no stone is erected to mark his grave, notwithstanding the many pledges made by the people of Illinois, irrespective of party, to his bereaved family before his burial, that his remains should be appropriately honored were they but allowed to repose within the state of his adoption.

The Monument Association was formed eighteen months ago, for the purpose of carrying out the wish of the public by raising funds adequate for the erection of a suitable monument; but owing mainly to the extraordinary and melancholy condition of the country, it has proved impossible thus far to make any material collections sufficient to purchase the land and commence the work, as it would have doubtless been easy to do in times of peace and prosperity, having only accumulated about twenty-five hundred dollars. But the committee are assured from experience, that should the State make a donation, the people at large would then feel a confidence in the speedy success of the object, and would doubtless respond more liberally in making up any deficiency.

The undersigned committee earnestly appeal to the legislators of the State to vote an appropriation to aid them in the immediate accomplishment of this noble purpose.

To carry out the plans of the association, the sum of $25,000 for the purchase of land, and $50,000 for the erection of the monument, is desired from the State.

It should not be said by the world that Illinois has forgotten her pledges, made over his dead body, and that the grave of him whose whole life was spent in her service, must go uncared for, without a single stone to record those eminent services, and mark the spot where he reposes.

The rearing of this tribute of respect to his memory should be done in part by the people, through their representatives, as such action would be alike honorable to the late Mr. Douglas, and to the State he so faithfully served; and this duty ought not to devolve upon his bereaved family, whose only inheritance was his illustrious name, and who have but recently been visited by another sad and irreparable loss in the death of a father and protector, to whose affectionate care they had been confided.

  Very Respectfully,
   Your obedient servants,
    THOMAS B. BRYAN, 1st Vice President,
    JOHN B. TURNER, 2nd Vice President,
    DAVID A. GAGE, Treasurer,
    JAMES DUGGAN, Bishop of Chicago,
    FRANCIS C. SHERMAN, Mayor of Chicago,
    LEONARD W. VOLK, Secretary.

The following advertisement was published in the Chicago papers:

At a meeting of the trustees of The Douglas Monument Association, held on the 23d instant, the executive committee were authorized to procure a design for the proposed monument, the cost of which not to exceed $50,000. The design or designs to be submitted on or before the 25th of March next, it being the intention of the trustees to commence the work immediately after adopting a plan, with as little delay as possible.

A sum not to exceed seventy-five dollars ($75) will be paid for the plan adopted, and the committee will not be responsible for any design or designs that may get injured or lost.

In this connection it is ordered by the committee that all agents of the association are hereby earnestly requested to make immediate returns to the association of all moneys which they may have collected, and those agents who cannot further act in behalf of the above object are requested to return their commissions, diplomas, &c., belonging to the association.

The friends of this cause, in all parts of the country, who will give information to the association of any collections made by authorized persons or otherwise, and not forwarded by them, will render a great service to the society, and which will be duly appreciated by the public.

      F. C. SHERMAN,
      D. A. GAGE,
      JOHN B. TURNER,
      JAMES DUGGAN,
       Executive Committee.

CHICAGO, January 25. 1864.

An adjourned meeting of the Board of Trustees was held at the Sherman House July 14, 1864, for the purpose of selecting a design for the proposed monument. There were present at the meeting, Messrs. Thos. B. Bryan, Right Rev. Bishop Duggan, Rev. Wm. Barry, D. A. Gage, S. W. Fuller, John M. Douglas, W. C. Goudy and F. C. Sherman. Mr. Bryan, First Vice President, occupied the chair, and Mr. Gage, Treasurer, acted as Secretary. There were but two competing designs presented—both models. After discussing the merits and practicability of the designs submitted, a ballot was taken resulting in the adoption of the design of Leonard W. Volk, by seven affirmative votes to one negative. The design will be described further on.

During the legislative session of 1864-5, the following bill was drawn by Mr. Goudy, of the association, and introduced by Col. A. F. Stevenson, member of the House of Representatives, and through whose indefatigable efforts passed both branches of the Legislature.

AN ACT TO APPROPRIATE TWENTY-FIVE THOUSAND DOLLARS TO PURCHASE THE TRACT OF LAND IN WHICH REPOSE THE REMAINS OF STEPHEN A. DOUGLAS.

SEC. 1. Be it enacted by the people of the State of Illinois, represented in the General Assembly, that the Governor of the State of Illinois is hereby authorized to purchase, in the name of the State of Illinois, the lot of ground in which now repose the remains of STEPHEN A. DOUGLAS, deceased, to-wit: Lot one (1) of the lower tier of Oakenwald subdivision of part of the south half of the north-east quarter of section 34, township 39 north, range 14 east, in the city of Chicago, Cook county, Illinois, and now owned by Mrs. A. Douglas; the same to be held as a burying place for said deceased, and for no other purpose; and the sum of twenty-five thousand dollars, or such less sum as may be required, is hereby appropriated out of any unappropriated money in the treasury. And, upon the certificate of the Governor as to the amount required, and that he has received an abstract of title and a proper deed, conveying the fee of the above described premises, as herein required, being presented to the Auditor of

Public Accounts, **he shall draw** his warrant for the amount thus **certified to, as a full** payment of the consideration money for the conveyance as aforesaid; and the Governor is hereby requested to **pay such sum** of money, appropriated as above, to Mrs. A. Douglas, **and to no other** person, whatsoever.

SEC. 3. This act shall be deemed a public act, and shall take effect and be in force from and after its passage.

Approved February 16, 1865.

UNITED STATES OF AMERICA, }
    STATE OF ILLINOIS, } ss.

I, Sharon Tyndale, Secretary of State of the State of Illinois, do hereby **certify** that the foregoing is a true copy of an enrolled law now on file in my office.

In witness whereof I have hereunto set my hand, and the great seal of State, at the city of Springfield, this 22nd day of March, A. D. 1865.

[Great Seal of the State of Illinois.]

        SHARON TYNDALE, Sec'y **of State.**

REPORT OF LEGISLATIVE PROCEEDINGS FEB. 3D, 1865.

PURCHASE OF THE GRAVE OF DOUGLAS.

THE finance committee **made** two reports upon the proposed appropriation of $25,000 for the purchase of the grounds in which sleep the remains of Stephen A. Douglas. Messrs. Noble, Huntly, Strevell, McIntyre and Hill sign the majority report, which is adverse to the appropriation, and Messrs. Platt, Logan, Morrill and Patten present the views of the minority in its favor.

The majority report is, in brief, as follows: That, while the government is engaged in subduing the rebellion, it is the duty of all good citizens to dedicate themselves and every available means within their control to the support of that government, leaving minor **objects to be adjusted until** after the war; and that, until **that time, our** patriot dead, both heroes and statesmen, will remain enshrined in the hearts of the people.

The minority report expresses the opinion: "That the state of Illinois should own the ground wherein repose the remains of Senator Douglas. No man ever claimed a home in Illinois who did more for the state than he who now sleeps his last sleep on the shores of Lake Michigan. While living, it was his pride to make Illinois in fact what was conceded to her in prospect—the glory of the republic. As a statesman, none in his day claimed to be his superior, while all parties drank of his wisdom and honored him as a devoted patriot.

"At his death his devoted wife desired to remove his remains to Washington, there to be interred in the national burying ground, where all could claim the privilege of bowing at the tomb of America's noble son, and all do honor, regardless of the claims of Illinois, who gave him to the world.

"But our noble Governor interfered, and besought his afflicted wife to permit the remains to slumber in his adopted state, that Illinois might do honor to his memory. She yielded to Illinois, and the remains were buried in his own beautiful Oakenwald.

"It is well known that Senator Douglas left but little for the support of his family. His young and accomplished wife and two noble boys were rich in the honors of their noble husband and parent, but poor in the means of worldly support; and, for the purpose of relieving their present necessities, Mrs. Douglas has consented to part with the ground where sleep the remains of her beloved husband, and deed it to Illinois, for the sum of $25,000. The state, in our judgment, ought to own this sacred soil. The state, in our judgment, ought to relieve their present wants; and we, therefore, feeling a state pride in this matter, have no hesitation in recommending this general assembly to purchase the ground so generously offered."

On motion of Mr. Stevenson, of Cook, the subject was made the special order for Monday afternoon at 2 o'clock.

By the following letter of Governor Oglesby to Mrs. Douglas, it will appear that the action of the State of Illinois in reference to the purchase of the burial place of her lamented statesman has been consummated. It is an act creditable to our State:

STATE OF ILLINOIS, EXECUTIVE DEPARTMENT,
SPRINGFIELD, April 5, 1865.

MRS. ADELE DOUGLAS, Washington City, D. C.:

DEAR MADAM: Your notice of the 6th ultimo was received some days ago, with the deed to lot one, in Oakenwald, Chicago,

Cook County, Illinois. Herewith I enclose you exchange on New York for $25,000, as requested.

I take the liberty to inclose you an authenticated copy of the Act of the Legislature of this State, which refers to the same subject.

I take pleasure in informing you that all the forms have been complied with, proper and necessary to vest in the State of Illinois the title to the ground upon which lie buried, in that State he loved so well and honored so long, the sacred remains of your devoted husband and Illinois' noble *patriot* and *statesman*. Always jealous of his immortal fame, the people of Illinois would not be satisfied to suffer the soil of his last home on earth to fall a heritage to any other than their own descendants.

With assurances of the highest personal esteem, I am, most respectfully, your obedient servant,

RICHARD J. OGLESBY,
Governor of Illinois.

STATEMENT OF THE TREASURER AND SECRETARY— RECEIPTS—EXPENDITURES—MEMBERSHIP.

THE following report of the past action and present condition of the Douglas Monument Association has just been presented by Messrs. D. A. Gage, treasurer, and L. W. Volk, secretary:

On behalf of the board of trustees of the Douglas Monument Association, and for the information of the public, the treasurer and secretary would respectfully make a brief statement of the affairs of the society—more particularly of the funds collected and expended since its organization.

The cash receipts to February 13, 1865, amount to the total sum of seven thousand five hundred and ten ($7,510.94) dollars, including two hundred and ten ($210) dollars interest allowed by the treasurer.

The expenditures to same date, three thousand eight hundred and ninety-five ($3,895.29) dollars, leaving a balance of cash in the treasury of three thousand six hundred and fifteen ($3,615.65) dollars, a gain since the last published statement of one thousand eight hundred and ninety ($1,890.37) dollars, which latter sum was nearly all obtained at Douglas' grave, from the sale of pictures.

The expenditures would appear unduly large, without being explained by the fact that nearly the entire amount received has been from the sale of engravings of Douglas, diplomas of membership, photographs of the monument, etc., all of which have cost a large proportion of the **amount paid out,** together with the commissions to agents for **selling** them. But few *bona fide* cash subscriptions, comparatively, have ever **been made to** this object, an equivalent of some kind having in most cases been given to the subscribers, who **have desired** to purchase a picture of some kind as a memento of Douglas, or of their visit to his grave, and the profits on such subscriptions or purchases now mainly constitute the fund in the treasury.

Therefore, the amount chiefly expended has been **for the purchase** of engravings of Douglas, diplomas of membership, photographs of the monument, and for printing of pamphlets and circulars, and also office furniture and rent.

Of the amount expended, the secretary has received altogether during over three years, for services, seven hundred and sixty-nine ($769.70) dollars. No expenses have been incurred for the past two years for fuel and lights, the same having been provided by the secretary without charge to the society, nor has any expenditures been made, as the vouchers filed in the office will show, except what was necessary to conduct the business of the association.

Besides the balance of cash, there are two valuable lots of land, situated near the grave of Douglas, donated and deeded to the association by the mother and sister of the late Mr. Douglas, to aid in the erection of the monument, and probably worth three thousand ($3,000) dollars.

It is expected that a few hundred dollars more may be in the hands of parties who have acted as agents in different parts of the country, and who are hereby requested to report immediately to the association any sums which they may hold, as every dollar that has been collected will soon be needed, with considerable besides, to enable the committee to make any material progress in the erection of the monument.

The society numbers seven honorary members of the board of trustees, two hundred and fifty honorary members of the association, two hundred and thirty-two of which were editors of newspapers, who paid for their membership by advertising the society's circular for a season in their papers; and two thousand eight hundred and five members of the association, in all three thousand and sixty-two members.

The Legislature of Illinois having, during its late session, made an appropriation for the purchase of the Douglas burial lot at Cottage Grove, in the southern limits of Chicago, it is to be hoped that the trustees of the Monument Association will soon hold a meeting and take energetic measures for increasing the fund and commencing work on the monument.

WARRANTY DEED OF THE SAID LOT TO THE STATE OF ILLINOIS.

"This indenture, made this first day of March, in the year of our Lord one thousand eight hundred and sixty-five (A. D. 1865), between Adele Douglas, widow of Stephen A. Douglas, deceased, late of Cook county, State of Illinois, party of the first part, and Richard J. Oglesby, Governor of the State of Illinois, and his successors in office, for the use and benefit of the people of the State of Illinois, of the second part: Witnesseth, that the said party of the first part, for and in consideration of the sum of twenty-five thousand dollars ($25,000), in hand paid by the said party of the second part, the receipt whereof is hereby acknowledged, and the said party of the second part forever released and discharged therefrom, has granted, bargained, sold, remised, released, conveyed, aliened and confirmed, and by these presents does grant, bargain, sell, remise, release, convey, alien and confirm unto the said party of the second part, and to his successors and assigns forever, all the following described lot, piece or parcel of land, situate in the county of Cook and State of Illinois, and known and described as follows, to wit: Lot one (1), in the lower tier of Oakenwald, subdivision (fronting on Woodland Park and Douglas Place) of a part of the south half of the northeast quarter of section thirty-four (34), township thirty-nine (39), north range fourteen (14), east of the third (3rd) principal meridian, in the city of Chicago, together with all and singular the hereditaments and appurtenances thereunto belonging or in anywise appertaining, and the reversion and reversions, remainder and remainders, rents, issues and profits thereof; and all the estate, right, title, interest, claim or demand whatsoever of the said party of the first part, either in law or equity, of, in and to the above bargained premises, with the hereditaments and appurtenances; to have and to hold the said premises above bargained and described, with the appurtenances, unto the said party of the second part, his heirs, successors and assigns forever.

And the said Adele Douglas, party of the first part, for herself, her heirs, executors and administrators, does covenant, grant, bargain and agree to and with the said party of the second part, his successors and assigns, that at the time of the unsealing and delivering of these presents, she is well seized of the premises above conveyed, as a good, sure, perfect, absolute and indefeasible estate of inheritance in law, in fee simple; and has good right, full power and lawful authority to grant, bargain, sell and convey the same in manner and form aforesaid: and that the same are free and clear from all former and other grants, bargains, sales, liens, taxes, assessments and incumbrances of what kind and nature soever; and the above bargained premises in the quiet and peaceable possession of the said party of the second part, his successors and assigns, against all and every other person or persons lawfully claiming or to claim the whole or any part thereof, the said party of the first part shall and will warrant and forever defend.

This deed being executed in conformity with an Act of the Legislature of the State of Illinois authorizing the Governor of said State to purchase the premises herein described, and the said Adele Douglas, party of the first part, hereby expressly waives and releases all right, benefit, privilege, advantage and exemption under or by virtue of any and all statutes of the State of Illinois, providing for the exemption of homesteads from sale on execution, or otherwise, and especially under the Act entitled "An Act to Exempt homesteads from sale on execution," passed by the General Assembly of the State of Illinois, A. D., 1857, and approved February 11, A. D. 1857, and an Act entitled "An Act to amend an Act entitled 'An Act to Exempt Homesteads from sale on execution,'" passed by said Assembly A. D. 1857, and approved February 17, A. D. 1857.

In witness whereof, the said party of the first part has hereunto set her hand and seal, the day and year first above written.

        [Signed]   ADELE DOUGLAS,

Signed, sealed and delivered in presence of

    [Signed]   JOHN S. HOLLINGSHEAD,
                        JOHN S. HOLLINGSHEAD, JR.

U. S. March, Internal Revenue. 1865. One Dollar. Mortgage. A. D. 10.	U. S. March, Internal Revenue. 1865. Five Dollars. Probate Will. A. D. Five.	U. S. March. Internal Revenue. 1865. Ten Dollars. Mortgage. A. D. 10.

DISTRICT OF COLUMBIA, } ss.
   Washington County,

I, John S. Hollingshead, a Notary Public in and for said county,

DOUGLAS COTTAGE, COTTAGE GROVE, BUILT 1853.

in the district aforesaid, do hereby certify that Adele Douglas, who is personally known to me to be the same person whose name is subscribed to the foregoing warranty deed, appeared before me this day, in person, and acknowledged that she signed, sealed and delivered the said instrument of writing as her free and voluntary act, for the uses and purposes therein set forth. Given under my hand and notarial seal, this sixth day of March, A. D. one thousand eight hundred and sixty-five (1865).

[L.S.]   [Signed]   JOHN S. HOLLINGSHEAD,
Notary Public, Washington County.

Early in the winter of 1866, the writer was authorized by the Trustees of the Association to locate the site of the monument, and in the performance of which duty he fixed it as nearly as he could remember on the precise spot which Senator Douglas pointed out to him in the summer of 1855, as the place whereon he intended to build his permanent residence.

At the time, the Senator was spending part of the summer in his little one-story frame cottage, standing among the primitive oaks in what is now known as Woodland Park, and which has, since his death, been moved by the writer, and which is occupied by him on Douglas Avenue adjoining the monument grounds. The design of the monument having been adopted as before stated, proposals were invited by advertisement for the construction of the foundations and tomb of Illinois limestone.

About a half-dozen sealed bids were received and opened by the building committee, consisting of Mayor F. C. Sherman, John B. Turner and D. A. Gage, and the contract was awarded to the lowest bidders at $10,700.

The work was begun immediately, and soon after preliminary steps taken to lay the corner stone with fitting ceremonies. The following action was taken by the Board of Trustees, by inviting the Hon. Wm. H. Seward, Secretary of State, to deliver an address upon the occasion.

LAYING OF THE CORNER-STONE.

To the Hon. William H. Seward,
Secretary of State, Washington:

Sir: The undersigned, the Board of **Trustees** of **The** Douglas Monument Association, would most respectfully **invite** you to be present and deliver the oration on the occasion **of laying the** corner-stone of the proposed monument, in honor of the **late Senator Douglas.**

Profoundly appreciating your eminent abilities as an **orator,** statesman and patriot, and **also** your personal acquaintance **with Mr. Douglas,** being cotemporaries in the Senate of the United States for so long a period, it is earnestly hoped that your public duties and health will permit you to accept the invitation hereby respectfully tendered.

It is the intention to lay **the** corner-stone **in the city of Chicago, on** the ground recently purchased **by the State of** Illinois, some time **during** the month of **May** or June **next.**

The Trustees would be **pleased,** however, **to** conform to your own convenience, as to the **precise day,** should you consent to confer upon them and the object **the honor of your** presence.

James Duggan,	John B. Turner,
William B. Ogden,	Thomas B. Bryan,
David A. Gage,	William C. Goudy,
John L. Wilson,	Samuel W. Fuller,
Wm. A. Richardson,	William Barry,
Samuel H. Treat,	John M. Douglas,
James C. Allen,	F. C. Sherman,
John D. Caton	John Dement,
Walter B. Scates,	

Leonard W. Volk, *Secretary.*

Chicago, March 22, 1866.

MR. SEWARD'S REPLY.

Department of State,
Washington, April 1, 1866.

To the Right Reverend James Duggan, D. D.,
And others, Chicago, Illinois:

Gentlemen:—I have **received** your **kind letter** of the 22d ultimo. It informs me of the purpose of the Douglas Monument Association to lay, in the month of May or June next, the corner-stone of the proposed monument in honor of the late Senator Douglas, and that the association has been pleased to invite me to deliver the oration on that occasion. In reply, I may inform you that I should consider it an agreeable duty to accept this invitation, which does not exaggerate the regard in which I hold the memory of Stephen A. Douglas. The last of his days in Washington were employed in consultation with President Lincoln and myself in organizing the resistance to disunion. Unless two events, which are now mentioned, should concur hereafter, I could not expect to be able to assume the proposed duty at a time so early as May or June. First, my returning health must become more distinctly established; second, official duties must become less exacting. At present, I am prevented, therefore, from making a promise which depends so materially upon the future for its realization.

Believe me to be, gentlemen, your very obedient servant,

WILLIAM H. SEWARD.

THE CORNER-STONE TO BE LAID ON THE 13TH OF JUNE—GOVERNOR OGLESBY TO DELIVER THE ORATION.

AN adjourned meeting of the board of trustees of the Douglas Monument Association was held at the Sherman House on the 11th May, 1866, Hon. John B. Turner, Second Vice President, in the chair, at which meeting several vacancies existing in the board were filled by the re-election of Walter B. Scates, S. M. Nickerson, and L. W. Volk, were also elected as trustees; the election of officers resulting as follows:

President—Walter B. Scates.
First Vice President—John B. Turner.
Second Vice President—John M. Douglas.
Treasurer—David A. Gage.
Secretary—Leonard W. Volk.
Executive Committee—W. B. Scates, President; J. B. Turner, First Vice President; F. C. Sherman; Right Rev. Bishop Duggan; D. A. Gage, Treasurer; L. W. Volk, Secretary.

The contract for the first section of the monument, comprising the foundations, platform steps and tomb, of Athens stone, having been let last October to Messrs. John Howison & Co. for the sum of $10,700, and the work thereon now progressing, the Treasurer was authorized to pay Messrs. Howison & Co. $1,000 on account of the work, in addition to a like sum paid them when the contract was executed.

The Hon. William H. Seward, who had been first invited to deliver the oration, but whose health and public duties prevented his acceptance so early as the present month of May or June next, the Governor of the State was then invited, and has consented to deliver the address.

A supplemental meeting of the board was held at the same place on the 13th instant, and Wednesday, the 13th day of June, was fixed upon for the dedication of the corner-stone of the monument. A Special Committee of four was selected from the Board of Trustees, consisting of Judge W. B. Scates, D. A. Gage, J. L. Wilson and L. W. Volk. Also, a Citizens' Committee of Arrangements was chosen, as follows:

Charles H. Walker, Esq., Geo. L. Dunlap, Esq., James W. Sheahan, Esq., General C. A. Dana, Wilbur F. Storey, Esq., Geo. W. Gage, Esq., Dr. B. McVickar, Col. J. L. Hancock, Col. Jas. H. Bowen, Hugh Maher, Esq., G. P. A. Healy, Esq., C. L. Woodman, Esq., Philip Wadsworth, Esq., Lieut.-Gov. Wm. Bross, Stephen Barrett, Esq., C. G. Wicker, Esq., Col. A. C. Hesing, H. D. Colvin, Esq., Rev. Dr. Dunne, D. D., J. C. Fargo, Esq., Hon Thomas Hoyne, Clinton Briggs, Esq., W. F. Coolbaugh, Esq., M. C. Stearns, Esq., Isaac R. Diller, Esq.

Another vacancy still existing in the Board of Trustees, Mr. Charles R. Starkweather was duly elected to fill the same.

The meeting then adjourned, subject to the call of the special committee.

The above committees are requested to meet at the Tremont House, on Tuesday evening, May 22nd, at 8 o'clock, to make the necessary arrangements for laying the corner-stone of the Douglas monument.

COMMENTS OF THE CHICAGO TIMES.

"HAD Congress, instead of inviting Bancroft to deliver a eulogy on Mr. Lincoln, invited Fernando Wood, Mr. Long, of Ohio, Mr. Harris, of Maryland, or any other democrat who had shown himself to be an extreme and bitter partisan, the action would have excited such intense indignation among republicans that the invitation would, very probably, have been rescinded. It would have appeared as a studied and intentional insult to the memory of Mr. Lincoln and to his political friends and the party of which he was a member and which elected him to the presidency. For this reason, either of the three last gentlemen named would have declined the invitation. Their sense of propriety, their deference to usage, their conciousness that their political prejudices unfitted them to grasp impartially the considerations which influenced the action of Mr. Lincoln, and their respect for the feelings of political opponents, would all have commanded them to decline appearing on such an occasion to eulogize him they had so often and warmly opposed.

"The Douglas Monument committee has invited Governor Oglesby to deliver the address at the laying of the corner-stone of the monument. The invitation can only be excused on the supposition that the committee is ignorant of usage and of propriety. The governor has accepted the invitation, which is one of the best evidences that could be given that he is unfit to perform the honorable task required. He knows that he is a leader in that party which pursued Douglas with bitterest hatred from the time it came into being until he died, and that mobbed him in this city and within sight of the ground where his bones lie and where the monument is to be built. You, gentlemen of the committee, and you Richard J. Oglesby, will do well to reconsider the invitation and its acceptance. If you have no respect for the party of which Douglas was leader, and to which rightly belongs the controlling voice in paying him posthumous honors, you may refrain from insulting his memory by the selection of one of his bitterest enemies during his whole life to officiate on such an occasion."

An adjourned meeting of the committee of citizens appointed to make arrangements for laying the corner-stone of the Douglas monument, was held in parlor No. 1, of the Tremont House, last evening. The attendance was very full, and Judge Walter B. Scates presided.

The chairman stated, for the benefit of those not present at the last meeting, the objects for which the committee had convened.

The sub-committee, to whom was referred the arrangements of the inauguration, the laying down of plans of action, and the ceremonies to be observed, reported through their chairman, Col. J. H. Bowen, as follows :

"Your committee, appointed at the meeting on the 22nd inst., to devise some plan for the furtherance of the object of the committee of arrangements, namely, the laying of the corner-stone of the Douglas Monument with appropriate and as imposing ceremonies as may be possible, would respectfully submit the following recommendations, unanimously adopted by your committee:

1st. The time fixed upon by the Trustees of the Monument Association is, in their judgment, too near at hand to make suitable preparations for the ceremonies, and they are of opinion that the 4th day of July next would be the most fitting day for those services.

2d. That they deem it appropriate that the Masonic fraternity should lay the corner-stone, according to their usage in such cases.

3d. That the civic and military societies should be invited to participate.

4th. A committee of five on invitation should be selected to invite leading and distinguished public men and organized bodies on the occasion.

Also a committee on finance, to provide for such contingent expenses as may be incurred, without encroaching upon the monument fund.

5th. That the Hon. John B. Rice, Mayor of Chicago, be appointed President of the day, and David A. Gage, Esq., Marshal of the day.

Signed by the committee.

The report of the committee was considered *seriatim*, and was adopted, after which the committee was discharged.

A communiation was received from Gov. Oglesby stating his inability to be present at the ceremonies, if held on the fourth day of July, having made an engagement elsewhere for that day which was imperative.

L. W. Volk, secretary, asked to be excused from the duties as secretary of the citizens' committee, and, upon motion, his resignation was accepted, and H. W. Zimmerman was elected in his stead.

The Committee upon Invitations were selected as follows:

W. F. Coolbaugh, Col. J. H. Bowen, Hon. Thos. Hoyne, Charles Walker, and Dr. B. McVickar.

The following gentlemen were appointed a Committee on Finance:

H. D. Colvin, C. G. Wicker, M. C. Stearns, Clinton Briggs, A. C. Hesing, I. R. Diller, Philip Wadsworth.

C. L. Woodman moved that a committee of three be appointed to **invite the Masonic** fraternity to perform the ceremony of **laying the corner-stone.**

The **motion** prevailed, and the following gentlemen **were appointed such** committee:

L. W. Volk, I. R. Diller, and Col. J. H. Bowen.

The chairman and secretary were empowered to fill the vacancy of secretary to the committee in case the new appointee was unable to serve.

The chairman, **Judge Scates,** announced **his intention to be** absent a few days, and Charles Walker was appointed to act in his stead **during his absence.**

The Committee on Invitation was instructed **to procure an orator for the** occasion, selecting such person as **they, in their discretion,** might think proper.

The Committee on Finance was instructed to meet at the office of Col. I. R. Diller on Saturday afternoon, **at** 3 o'clock.

C. G. Wicker moved **that all** organizations **and societies desiring to join in the procession be** instructed **to report to** the Chief Marhal. The **motion prevailed.**

The committee then adjourned until 8 o'clock **P. M.** on Thursday next.

LETTER FROM GOV. OGLESBY.

Springfield, Ill., May 28, 1866.

Colonel James H. Bowen, Chicago, Ill.:

Dear Colonel: Your letter of the 23d inst., for some reason, did not reach me until to-day, too late to reply for any purpose connected with the special inquiries you make: "If it will suit me to make the address on the 4th of July instead of on the 13th of June, the time fixed by the Trustees of the Douglas Monument Association for laying the corner-stone of the monument to the late Senator Douglas. After having made a written promise to speak in Marion county on the 4th of next July, it was not possible for me to reply to Mr. Volk or yourself, on the 23d inst., that I could positively agree to the change on that day; but it seems my telegraphic reply to Mr. Volk to do with it—as the change was nevertheless made on that day to the 4th of July. It is thus very clear to my mind that I am disposed of. The Chicago *Times* of the 24th made a very severe attack upon me for accepting the invitation to deliver the address. It is not, perhaps, known that I was twice urgently invited to do so before accepting, and I suppose when the attack in the *Times* appeared that the trustees would be generous enough to me to make the explanation which obviously seemed necessary. I am thus left in a disagreeable relation to the whole matter. I declined as long as I gracefully could, then, after accepting, am virtually rejected by a change of time, arbitrarily and very suddenly made. If the Masons are to lay the corner-stone, why prefer the 4th of July to the 24th of June—this year the 25th—a Masonic day. The trustees have not informed me whether they expect me to deliver the address or not. I think I am able to comprehend why!

Very respectfully yours,

R. J. OGLESBY.

EXPLANATORY LETTER.

To the Editor of the Chicago Evening Journal:

I desire, on behalf of the Board of Trustees of the Douglas Monument Association, to state some facts, as they appear on the records, for the information of the public relating to the invitation of Governor Oglesby to deliver the address on the occasion of laying the corner-stone of the Douglas Monument.

In the first place, the Board thought best to invite Secretary Seward, the correspondence with whom has been already published in the papers. Failing to secure that gentleman, it was then decided to invite the Governor of the State, His Excellency Richard J. Oglesby, who, it was known, was a friend of the object of the Association, and had exerted his influence in securing the appropriation from the State for the purchase of the grounds upon which lie the remains of Mr. Douglas. The Governor declined to deliver the adress. He said: "I am concious of inability to do justice, upon such an occasion, to the life, the character and public services of this great man." He expressed a purpose, however, to be present as a spectator.

At a full meeting of the Board, held soon after the receipt of his letter, it was unanimously decided that a member thereof should write to the Governor urging him to reconsider his action in declining, and to fix any day for the occasion prior to the 15th of June. The letter was written, and the Governor replied that he did not feel longer at liberty to decline, and stated that any day after the 12th of June would be agreeable to him to make the address.

The Board, at its next meeting, fixed upon the 13th instant for laying the stone, and the Governor was notified of the fact by telegraph.

At this meeting, a citizens' committee of arrangements was appointed, together with a special committee of five members from the board to represent it, and co-operate with the citizen's committee in making all necessary preparations for the dedication ceremonies.

The committee of arrangements thus appointed deemed a change of the day to the 4th of July important. As Governor Oglesby had signified that any day after the 12th of June would suit his convenience, it was thought that his services could still be secured but, in this, the committee have been disappointed, because of a prior engagement of the Governor to deliver an address at Salem on that day.

At a recent meeting of the Committee on Invitations, consisting of Messrs. William F. Coolbaugh, Thomas Hoyne, James H. Bowen, Charles Walker, and Brock McVickar, the following resolution was passed:

"*Resolved*, That this committee, charged with the duty of securing the services of some gentleman to deliver an appropriate address on the Fourth of July next, on the occasion of laying the corner-stone of the monument about to be erected to the memory of the late Stephen A. Douglas, convey to Governor Oglesby their regret that his engagements will prevent his being present and performing that service; and while they feel the necessity, in view of the Governor's declination, of securing some other gentleman, respectfully request, if any change of his arrangements will allow of it, his presence on that occasion."

In view of the above facts, the Committee on Invitations are using every endeavor to secure some gentleman as orator on the proposed occasion, who will be eminently qualified and satisfactory to all.

LEONARD W. VOLK,
Secretary Douglas Monument Association.

At a subsequent meeting of the Citizens' Committee of Arrangements, Messrs. Thos. Hoyne and Jas. H. Bowen were appointed a committee to proceed to Washington and invite the President of the United States, his Cabinet, and other prominent men to be present at the ceremonies. Gen. John

A. Dix was secured by the committee as the orator. He came to Chicago some days in advance of the Presidential party to prepare his address.

The Special Committee of The Douglas Monument Association held a meeting last evening at the rooms of the association, No. 15 Garrett Block. Present—General Walter B. Scates, President, and all the members of the committee.

Mr. David A. Gage, from the Committee on Railroads, reported that he had seen the presidents of all the railroads running into the city, except two, and that they had agreed to carry passengers to the city and back at the reduced rate of one and one-fifth the usual fare. The two roads which were not yet in the arrangement were the Chicago and Great Eastern, and the Chicago, Pittsburgh and Fort Wayne.

Mr. Volk, from the Committee on Medals, reported in favor of a circular, white metal badge of the diameter of one and three-eighths inches, and with a hole near the margin to admit of a ribbon. On one side of the medal was to be a medalion of Douglas, surrounded on the rim with the words,

"BORN, APRIL 23, 1813; DIED, JUNE 3, 1861."

On the reverse, the words,

"DOUGLAS MONUMENT ASSOCIATION,"

Were to be upon the rim, and in the centre the words,

"CORNER-STONE LAID SEPT. 6, 1866."

A suitable medalion has already been provided, taken from the bust of Douglas. The cost would be from $10 to $15 per hundred, and if ordered immediately, five thousand could be made ready by September 1, and one thousand each day thereafter. The report of the committee was adopted.

Mr. Hilton proposed that, instead of the proposed banquet, there be held a reception at the Rink on the evening of the President's arrival.

A further suggestion was also made that a concert be held at the Opera House on the evening of September 6. Both the above suggestions were referred to the general committee, with favorable recommendations, to be reported upon this evening.

Mr. Volk proposed that the seal of the association be put upon a badge for the exclusive use of the Committee of Arrangements. It was adopted.

Mr. Coolbaugh proposed that a committee of two be appointed

by the chairman, who should appoint a Reception Committee of fifty, who shall proceed to Detroit, or some place this side, to receive the President and his suite.

The Chairman appointed Chas. Walker, Esq., and Dr. Brock McVickar, who reported the following as the Special Reception Committee:

Richard J. Oglesby, Governor, William Bross, Lieutenant Governor, Lyman Trumbull, United States Senator, Richard Yates, United States Senator, John Wentworth, M. C., A. C. Hesing, E. B. Washburn, M. C., P. H. Smith, Esq., E. C. Ingersoll, M. C., I. Y. Munn, H. P. H. Bromwell, M. C., Charles Randolph, L. W. Ross, M. C., Clinton Briggs, S. S. Marshall, M. C., Henry Greenebaum, A. J. Kuykendall, M. C., General Osborn, J. F. Farnsworth, M. C., Judge Thos. Drummond, A. C. Harding, M. C., J. H. Woodworth, B. C. Cook, M. C., C. N. Holden, S. M. Cullom, M. C., E. B. McCagg, Esq., Anthony Thornton, M. C., W. H. Brown, Jehu Baker, M. C., M. C. Stearns, S. W. Moulton, M. C., M. D. Ogden, Esq., Hon. Leonard Sweet, E. D. Taylor, Esq., Hon. I. N. Arnold, D. Kreigh, L. D. Boone, H. D. Colvin, Hon. J. Y. Scammon, Hon. J. B. Rice, J. C. Dore, General Mann, Judge E. VanBuren.

TRUSTEES OF THE DOUGLAS MONUMENT ASSOCIATION, AND OF THE UNIVERSITY OF CHICAGO.

Prof. J. C. Borroughs, Hon. F. C. Sherman, Hon. Julian Rumsey, C. G. Wicker, J. R. Jones, Colonel R. M. Hough.

The Secretary made a statement of the persons and classes, to whom invitations have been extended. He said the number of invitations already sent out numbered more than 800, and embraced the following:

President of the United States and the Cabinet.
Both houses of Congress.
Judges of the Supreme Court of the United States.
Judges of the Supreme Courts of the several States.
Mayors of all the cities in the Northwest.
Editors of the leading papers of the United States.
Many other distinguished statesmen and journalists.
Generals Grant and Sherman.

Messrs. Volk, Zimmerman and Gage were appointed a committee to request the Board of Trustees of the association to prepare suitable records and mementos to be placed in the corner-stone.

Mr. Wadsworth moved that suitable arrangements be made with the proprietors of the Sherman House for the reception and entertainment of the President and suite.

Mr. D. A. Gage announced that the hospitalities of the Sherman House had already been freely tendered to the party. A vote of thanks was tendered to Mr. Gage.

It was stated that the Illinois Central Railroad would run trains to the grounds every ten minutes on the day of laying the corner-stone.

Badges are to be provided, one, selling for $2, and admitting both to the reception and the concert, and another costing $1, admitting only to the latter.

The meeting of the general committee of arrangements of the Douglass Monument Association, which was to have taken place to-night, has been postponed until to-morrow evening, same time and place, on account of the reception of General John A. Logan occurring to-night.

DISPATCH FROM SECRETARY SEWARD.

A TELEGRAM containing the following has just been received by S. C. Hough, Esq., general passenger agent of the Michigan Southern Railroad:

WASHINGTON, D. C., August 8.

The President, with his Cabinet, expect to reach Chicago on Wednesday, September 5th, at 7:45 in the evening, and remain there two nights and one day.

(Signed)   WILLIAM H. SEWARD.

THE PREPARATIONS FOR THE EVENT APPROACHING COMPLETION.

THE preparations for the approaching ceremonies attendant upon laying the corner-stone of the Douglas Monument, are rapidly approaching completion. All the preliminary arrangements are perfected, and little now remains but the preparation of the programme of the day. It will be remembered that at the last meeting of the general committee of arrangements, it was decided to abandon the Rink and request the use of the Hall of the Board of Trade, for the purposes of the Presidential Reception on the night of the 5th proximo. The Board of Directors have kindly consented to suspend their rules on this occasion, and to grant the use of their building to the association. The hall will be thrown open to the public on that occasion, and will be beautifully decorated in honor of the event. It was the original intention of the President and suite to have reached Chicago by the Michigan Southern route. Circumstances have, however, changed that part of the programme, and he will now travel by way of Detroit and the Michigan Central road, visiting Niagara Falls on his journey. Hearing of this intention, Mr. Swinyard, the superintendent of the Great Western railroad of Canada, sent an invitation to the President, in which he was joined by the Governor General, asking him to accept a special train over that road. The following is a copy of the correspondence.

Hamilton, Aug. 17, 1866.

"Hon. W. H. Seward, Secretary of State, Washington, D. C.:

"It is reported that the President, yourself and party will be at Niagara Falls at the beginning of September, *en route* for Chicago. If it should be consistent with the programme of the President and agreeable to his wishes, the Great Western Company will have the greatest possible pleasure in placing a special train over its road, from Niagara Falls to Detroit, at the service of himself and party. I was directed by His Excellency, the Governor, to say that it would give him the highest gratification to hear that the President, yourself and party would pass through Canada.

[Signed.]   "Thomas Swinyard."

"Washington, Aug. 18, 1866.

"Thomas Swinyard, Esq., Hamilton, C. W.:

"*My Dear Sir:* I give you many thanks for your telegram of yesterday, which informed me of the friendly reception which awaits the President and myself, if we should find it convenient to pass through Canada on our way to Chicago.

"I regret to say that definite arrangements for the journey preclude our acceptance of your kind invitation.

"Faithfully yours,

[Signed.]   "Wm. H. Seward."

[From the Chicago Tribune.]

ARTICLES TO BE DEPOSITED UNDER THE CORNER-STONE—THE MEDAL.

Mr. Volk, Secretary of the Douglas Monument Association, received yesterday a set of coins and medals from the mint at Philadelphia, which will be deposited, together with other articles in the corner-stone of the monument, on the sixth proximo. The coins embrace the dollar in gold, all the silver coins of the United States, and the five, three, two and one cents in composition, being all of the present year. The medals are the small Jackson and Washington mint medals, the two Washington medals known as the "Commission resigned" and "Time increases his fame," in silver, and a Washington medal struck to commemorate the taking of the oath of allegiance by the employes of the mint, in bronze; also the Lincoln and Johnson Indian medals in bronze. They are mainly pattern pieces, and are extremely sharp and beautiful. The medals struck by Mr. Childs, of this city, of Lincoln and Douglas, from Mr. Volk's busts, during the campaign, will also be deposited in the stone.

The following are the other articles which will be deposited in the corner-stone: Specimens of United States paper money; records of the Douglas Monument Association; a copper plate with the names of Trustees engraved thereon; pamphlet, by-laws, constitution and appeal; diploma of membership, blank circulars, agents' credentials, etc., of the association; medallion of Douglas, with date of the laying of the stone; photograph of the monument; likeness of Douglas on porcelain, together with a photograph; Sheahan's Life of Douglas, to 1858; last speeches of the great statesman before the Illinois Legislature and in the Wigwam; his funeral ceremonies in 1861; obituary addresses in the Senate and House of Representatives; eulogy before the University; miscellaneous documents relating to Douglas; copy of Douglas' deed of land to the University of Chicago; copy of each of the daily city papers; copy of *Harpers' Weekly*, with the monument illustrated; first and last copies of the catalogues of the University; Douglas' ancestral record; statistics of the Chamber of Commerce of Chicago, first and last Directories of Chicago; copies of the catalogues of the Art Exhibitions in Chicago in 1859, 1863 and 1865;

charter of the Chicago **Historical Society; and an autograph letter of the deceased.**

We saw, yesterday, a proof of the medal struck to commemorate the occasion, by order of the **committee. It is** from Mr. Child's dies. The obverse side has **a very** accurate bust portrait **of Douglas from** Volk's bust, clear, sharp and very expressive. **Of all the medals** which have been struck in commemoration of Douglas and his services, some ninety **in number,** this is by far the best. The inscription on **the obverse is,** "Born April 23, 1813, died June 3, 1861," with three **stars below the** bust. The reverse **bears** the inscription, "**Douglas Monument** Association, **Corner** Stone laid Sept 6, 1866," **with** a single **star** in the exergue. **The** medal is in white **metal and is** very neat.

The impression has gained ground in some quarters that the **Masonic fraternity** will not take part in the ceremonies. This impression is false. The **Grand** Master **of the State will** attend in person, and many of **the different** lodges **of the State, with nearly all** those of Chicago, have **already** signified **their intention to be present.**

The number of flags procured for draping purposes is very large, **embracing** probably the great majority of those owned in the city. **The display** will doubtless be a magnificent one.

The **city council of** St. **Paul,** Minnesota, **has** appointed Mayor **Prince, General Sibley,** Hon. J. B. Brisbin, Messrs. McCarty and **Howard, and Alderman** Beaumont, delegates to attend the Douglas **monument** ceremonies. **It is** understood that the treasury of that city is too much impoverished **to** admit **of** their expenses being paid by the corporation.

THE PRESIDENTIAL PARTY.

The following distinguished persons constitute **the** President's **party,** according **to** the telegrams received by the **chief** marshal. There are, however, some eighty persons accompanying, whose names are not furnished, and who are consequently not regarded as coming within the province of the committee **of** reception to specially entertain:

President Johnson and servant; General U. S. Grant **and servant; Maj.** General **Geo. G.** Meade; Brigadier J. A. **Rawlings; Admiral** Farragut, lady **and** servant; Secretary Seward and servant; **Major** Seward; Secretary **Welles, lady and two sons;** Senor **Romero; General** McCullum; Surgeon-General Barnes; Surgeon **Norris, U. S. N.; Rear** Admiral Radford, **U. S. N.;** Lieutenant

Gurley, U. S. N.; Colonel W. G. Moore; Colonel R. Morrow; I. A. Gobright; W. W. Warden; J. R. Doolittle; R. S. Spafford; General Steadman; General Rousseau; Mr. Palte; Mr. Kuntz; General Custer; H. A. Chadwick; H. Murphy; D. F. Patterson and lady; Marshal Gooding; Marshal D. Perrine; J. McGinnis and lady; Miss Grier; Masters Robert and Stephen A. Douglas, and Mrs. J. M. Grau and Mrs. J. N. Granger, only sister of Judge Douglas.

From this time on, till the arrival of the distinguished party, many committee meetings were held, and all arrangements made to make the occasion worthy of the departed senator and honorable to the state.

[From the Chicago Times.]

THE CHIEF MARSHAL'S ORDER OF ARRANGEMENTS.

The various societies and civil bodies that have not yet reported will report to Chief Marshal Gage at the Sherman House, under whose superintendence the procession will commence forming at 9 o'clock.

First division will form on Lake street, right resting on Wabash avenue.

Second division will form on Clark street, right resting on Randolph street.

Third division will form with right resting on the left of second division.

Fourth division will form on Dearborn street, right resting on Lake street.

Fifth division will form with right resting on the left of fourth division.

Sixth division will form on Dearborn street.

The following is the order of the procession as determined upon by the chief marshal and his associates:

ORDER OF PROCESSION.

Section of Police under Capt. Hickey.
Chief Marshal David A. Gage, Esq; L. P. Bradley, Philip Wadsworth, J. C. Hilton, Col. John Mason Loomis, Aids.

DOUGLAS MONUMENT.

FIRST DIVISION.

Band.
Masonic Fraternity.
Grand Marshal, Gen. A. C. Ducat and Aids.

SECOND DIVISION.

Band.
Gen. Manu and Aids.
President of the United States, Orator of the Day, Mayor Rice and Hon. W. H. Seward, in first carriage.
The Cabinet and other distinguished guests in carriages.
United States Army Officers—Gen. Grant, Gen. Rawlins, Gen. Meade and Staff, Gen. Steadman, Gen. Rousseau, Gen. Custer, Gen. Jeff. C. Davis, Gen. Crook, Gen. G. H. Thomas, in carriages.
United States Navy Officers—Admiral Farragut, Admiral Radford, Lieut. McKinley.
Trustees of the Douglas Monument Association in carriages.
Members of the Grand Lodge of T. & A. M. of Illinois, in carriages.
Citizen's Committee of Arrangements on foot.
Common Council of Chicago.
Mayors and Councils of Sister Cities on foot.

THIRD DIVISION.

Band.
Maj. C. H. Dyer.
Twenty-third and Seventy-second Regiments of Illinois Volunteers.
Division Marshal, David Walsh, Ald. John A. Moore.
Hibernian Benevolent Society.
French Benevolent Society.
United Sons of Erin.
Union National Society of Italians.
Father Matthew Temperance Society.

FOURTH DIVISION.

Band.

Edmund Crossfield, **Marshal.**
Trades Unions of **Chicago.**

FIFTH DIVISION.
Band.
Charles Alexander Kadish, **Marshal.**
Bohemian Sclavonic **Society.**
Sclovaueka Lipa.
Sclavonian Brotherhood (Protestant).
St. Wenzealaus' Society (Catholic).
Local Turners' Society.
Alahoe Singers' Society.

SIXTH DIVISION.
Band.
Andrew Schall, Marshal.
Sharpshooters.
Union Singing Association.
German Turnverein.
Butchers' Association.
Citizens generally.

LINE OF MARCH.

The route to be taken has already been published in THE TIMES, but for purposes of reference we give it again. The right, forming on Clark street and resting upon Lake, will proceed down the latter street to Wabash avenue, thence south on Wabash avenue to Sixteenth street, thence east to Michigan avenue, thence south to Thirty-first street, thence east to Cottage Grove avenue, and south to the monument grounds.

THE CONCERT.

The concert at the opera house this evening will, it is expected, be a splendid affair. All the arrangements have been made under the superintendence of Mr. Balatka, which will be assurance enough of the character of the entertainment. Miss Sterling, a famous Eastern contralto singer, will give some of her choicest selections. The few Chicagoans who have had the good fortune to hear her, pronounce her singing most perfect. The Germania Maennerchoer will also sing their best selections, among them "Storck's Prayer Before the Battle" and the celebrated "Sailor's Chorus" from L'Africaine.

The orchestra will number 45 performers, and among other selections will give the brilliant overture to Robespierre, in which the Marseilles hymn is one of the principal themes, some symphonical compositions and Meyerbeer's splendid Schiller march.

THE PUBLIC OFFICES.

The United States custom house and depository will be closed at 10 o'clock on the 6th inst., in honor of the ceremonies.

The Board of Trade will hold no session, and the city banks will be closed. The wholesale houses will also, it is understood, be open but for a short time in the morning, though there is no positive agreement to that effect.

DISTINGUISHED ARRIVALS.

Maj. Gen. Jeff. C. Davis, commander of the military department of Kentucky, arrived in the city on Tuesday evening to participate in the ceremonies of the day. While in the city he is the guest of E. L. Jansen, and Gen. A. C. McClurg, who was a member of his staff on the march through Georgia.

Sir Knight, Capt. Gaskin of Kingston, Canada, has been invited to join with the Chicago Masonic order in the reception of the President, and has accepted the invitation.

The following is a portion of the New York *Herald's* account of the journey to Chicago and the ceremonies at the grave:

THE REAL PURPOSE OF THE TRIP.

It was only upon our arrival in Chicago last night that we became really apprised of the nature of the Presidential trip. We find it actually to be for the purpose of attending the ceremonies of inaugurating a monument to the memory of a deceased statesman, and that it is not entirely a political excursion for partisan purposes. The idea prevailed that some turbulent spirits in Chicago seemed to view it in this light, and no little asperity of feeling was created thereby.

THE BOARD OF TRADE GUARDED.

According to the original programme the reception of the President of the United States and other distinguished visitors here was to take place in the hall of the Board of Trade. The majority of the members of this association participated in the ruffianly mob which a few years ago mobbed Douglas in the streets of Chicago, and when the Board of Directors was applied to for the use of the hall to receive the President of the United States and other distinguished persons visiting the city, they passed a resolution granting the use of the hall, but purposely omitted to mention the name of the President in the resolution. His friends felt the insult keenly, but deemed it prudent to say nothing. When the fact that the use of the hall had been granted for this purpose became known among certain persons in the board a regular storm of indignation was aroused and resolutions were drawn requesting the directors to rescind their former resolutions and refuse the hall, and other resolutions declaring that if the President made any political utterances in the hall it would be regarded as an insult.

After canvassing the matter for some time they came to the conclusion that such an insult to the President in advance of his coming would recoil upon their own heads, and so neither set of resolutions were offered. There was a general understanding among them, however, that they would attend the reception and come early enough to take possession of the hall, and then if the President said anything having a political bearing, they would lay violent hands on him and eject him from the hall by force. This determination was well understood by friends of the President, and while many of them were in favor of taking him to the Board of Trade hall and asking him to make a political speech, protect him in whatever he might say, at whatever cost and to whatever extreme it might be carried, other counsels prevailed, and the friends of the President concluded not to take him under the roof of his enemies. It was deemed to be more becoming to the dignity and honor of the nation that its Chief Magistrate should be received in the air, or the rotunda of a hotel, anywhere other than beneath the roof of the fanatics who mobbed Douglas. It was not known whether the President would desire to say anything relative to the politics of the country or not, but if he did not desire to do so his friends did not wish it said that the omission was due to the fact that he was afraid to speak upon this subject. Hence the place of reception was changed from the Board of Trade hall to the Rotunda of the Sherman House.

THE RADICAL INTERRUPTIONS AT CHICAGO.

The interruptions of the President last night, by vociferous cheers for Grant, originated at the radical *Tribune* office, opposite the Sherman House, and was re-echoed by the squads scattered in various parts of the immense crowd until a commanding voice cried, "Home." Then the interruptions ceased. This seemed to be the watchword of the turbulents, who had doubtless organized to prevent the President from being heard. They found, however, that he had more friends than they expected, as was the case at Toledo and Cleveland.

GENERAL STEEDMAN INSULTED AND REVENGED.

Toledo is the home of General Steedman. While he was saying a few words, same one in the crowd used some insulting language, when he was immediately silenced and hustled out by the General's friends.

THE PRESIDENT'S PURPOSES IN SPEAKING SO MUCH.

The President desires to make his policy known personally to the people. He thinks he can convince them that he is right and Congress wrong. Many of his friends, however, think he is only furnishing ammunition to his enemies, and while increasing their bitterness, is also spurring them to redoubled exertions.

GRANT REPORTED DISGUSTED.

It is reported that General Grant has said: "I am disgusted with this trip. I am disgusted at hearing a man make speeches on the way to his own funeral." It is reported that this was said in presence of a clerk in the employ of General Grant's brother, in this city, and other responsible parties. There are no indications, however, that the relations between the President and General Grant are not of an entirely harmonious character, although the General passes most of his time in other than the presidential car when traveling.

HOTEL ACCOMMODATIONS EN ROUTE.

The President's Private Secretary, Colonel Moore, has been very busy all the morning in dispatching official business, which has largely accumulated within a few days. At the Biddle House, in

Detroit, so poor were the arrangements for the accommodation of the party that at breakfast the President and his Cabinet officers were compelled to remain standing for a considerable time without a place to rattle a knife and fork. Half an hour elapsed before some of the party were waited upon. It is said that the colored waiters had struck and would not serve the President because he had vetoed the civil rights' bill. The case was entirely different at the Sherman House, in this city, where not only were the apartments prepared for the President and suite of the most elegant and *recherche* description, but the courteous attentions of the hosts all that could be desired. For the first time during the trip the President and the distinguished members of his party were entertained in a manner becoming their stations. The attention bestowed upon the President at the International Hotel, at Niagara, were also highly creditable to the management of the fashionable summer resort.

THE PROCESSION.

GRAND CROWDS FROM CITY AND COUNTRY—CHICAGO PACKED WITH STRANGERS—THE PARADE AND MARCH TO THE GROUNDS—SITE OF THE MONUMENT AND SCENE OF THE CEREMONIES.

As day dawned over the great metropolis, the time of preparation commenced, and long before the rising sun had chased the mists off the lake and gilded the steeples of the city, the streets were alive with the commotion of thousands of people. The various societies and organizations that were to participate in the ceremonies of the day were moving to their respective positions, with banners flying and bands of music preceding them. By eight o'clock every street visible from either balcony of the Sherman House presented a hurrying throng, which was continually increased by the arrival of regular and special trains bearing into the city countless thousands from the interior of all contiguous States. The different steamboat lines leading to the city were loaded to their utmost, and in most instances had been chartered for weeks beforehand to transport military companies and organizations that had been invited to attend. Private parties were made up weeks beforehand from all quarters of the country and had chartered cars, trains and steamboats for the great occasion. These generally brought with them their own music and some badge, or carried some banner to denote from whence they came and their common bond of union.

The number of visitors from abroad was variously estimated at from fifty thousand to one hundred thousand, with the probabilities decidedly in favor of the larger number. The mass of people in the city at ten o'clock was too great and extended to admit of much beyond conjecture, and by its mobility baffled all attempts at computation. The heavens were overcast and threatening, before the hour for moving the procession, and many were doubtless deterred by fear of rain and storm from joining its ranks. To others the change was agreeable, by promising a relief from the dreaded heat, and dust usually incident to such occasions. At an early hour in the morning ropes were stretched across Clark street, at its intersection with Randolph and Lake streets; a strong detail of police were on the ground, to prevent the multitude from passing the barricade, and the open space thus secured was kept comparatively clear from the intrusion of any, but those entitled to a place within. Notwithstanding these precautions, several hundred managed to elude the police in some way and kept increasing the crowd within until it was almost as densely packed as without. A company of zouaves did excellent service afterwards in clearing the square and keeping it open, and also attracted much attention by their splendid uniform and perfect evolutions.

APPEARANCE OF THE PRESIDENT.

Soon after ten o'clock the President was announced in readiness, and was handed into his carriage by the Grand Marshal of the day. As he emerged from the private enterance of the hotel, on Clark street, a shout of welcome and applause went up from the thousands assembled on the street and housetops that woke the echoes of lake and prairie.

EXCITING SCENES.

The scene at this moment was one of the most exciting ever witnessed. The music of bands, the cheering of the people, the waving of flags and handkerchiefs from windows, balconies and curbstones, made a grand tableau worthy of perpetuation. As the President's carriage passed on, and General Grant and his chief of staff, General Rawlins, mounted the steps of the second one, the applause swelled into a torrent that would have drowned the roar of Niagara itself. Next followed Admiral Farragut, at whose presence the inexhaustible enthusiasm of the populace re-**burst into such** rounds of applause **as can** only proceed from the throats of the stalwart sons of the West. As each member of the **party** known to the people by reputation passed through the line, the same uproar ensued, **until** the *cortege* **had passed** on and was followed by the various societies.

THE LINE OF MARCH

was crowded from curb-stone to roof, and many of **the private houses and all of the public buildings** were decorated **with flags and devices in** honor of the occasion.

THE PROCESSION

was imposing, and included **the** Masonic Fraternity, together with a force **of** police and the **chief** marshals and aids preceding the President of the United States, and **General Dix, the orator of the** day. Then **came** Mayor **Rice** and Hon. **William H. Seward,** the Cabinet and other distinguished guests; **United States Army officers,** General Grant, General Rawlins, **General** Meade and **Staff,** General Steedman, General **Rousseau, General** Custer, and **other** prominent officers; United States Navy officers—Admiral Farragut, Admiral Radford, Lieutenant McKinley; Trustees of the **Douglas Monument Association, members of the Grand** Lodge of **A. F. and A. M. of Illinois, in carriages;** citizens, committee of arrangements, **on foot; the Common Council of** Chicago, Mayors and Councils of sister cities on foot; Twenty-third and Sixty second regiments Illinois volunteers; Hibernian Benevolent Society, French Benevolent Society, United Sons of Erin, Union **National** Society, of Illinois; Father Matthew Temperance Society, Edmund Grossfield, marshal; Trades' Unions of Chicago, Charles Alexander Kadish, marshal; Bohemian Sclavonic Society, **Scalvonska Lipa** Brotherhood, Protestant St. Wenseeslaus **Society, Catholic Local Turners'** Society, Alahoe Singers Society, Andrew Schall, marshal; Sharpshooters' Union, Singing Society, German Turnverein, Butchers' **Association,** citizens generally.

AN OFFENSIVE DEMONSTRATION.

But one offensive demonstration was attempted, and that signally failed from its puerility. A Mrs. Sticknor, supposed to be a **widow,** residing at No. 42 Harrison street, had a large placard **on** the front of her house, "No Welcome to Traitors," and displayed a string of black petticoats across the front of the house below it. As Secretary Seward noticed the inscription he placed his hand grimly on the scars received by the assassins' knife, and looked inquisitively at his comrades in the carriage; General Grant and Admiral Farragut looked about them as though the mysterious handwriting on the wall was meant as a kindly warning that a Confederate army with banners was just around the corner ready to pounce upon and annihilate them. Others smiled complacently at the weakness of the procedure. The more charitable concluded the woman's husband had probably been hung as a rebel traitor by some of the patriotic generals in the procession, and that his weak-minded wife had thus indirectly paraded her private grief and unmentionable garments.

THE GROUNDS.

The procession reached Fairview, on the Douglas place, at twelve o'clock. This is the piece of ground which Mr. Douglas, in his life-time, purchased for the home of himself and family, in the anticipated years of life and honorable fame that lay before him. That same ground is now the place of his abode in death, and there the ceremonies of the day were performed to his memory under circumstances of peculiar solemnity.

THE CEREMONIES.

DESCRIPTION OF THE MONUMENT AND GROUNDS—IMPOSING CEREMONIES OF LOWERING THE STONE—NATURE ASSISTS AT THE CEREMONY—DECORATIONS OF THE GROUNDS.

ARRIVED on the ground the procession formed in the vicinity of the base of the monument. The grave was beautifully decorated. Four columns thirty-five feet in height stood at each corner of the grave, with arches rising thirty-four feet in the center, spanning from one to the other. These were festooned with draperies and flags of black cloth fringed with silver; while the columns were wound round with ornamental draperies interspersed with roses and evergreens.

On the top of each column and over the center of the arches

were urns and vases of flowers, etc. The fence around the grave was completely enshrouded with flags, so as to conceal it from view. The ground inside was strewn with wild flowers, and a marble bust of Douglas, with a model of the monument, were placed on pedestals near the head of the grave. The stands completely surrounded the tomb, and in the interval beyond these, far off to the boundaries of the Douglas estate, the audience was massed in solid ranks. The entire spectacle presented an amphitheatre, of which the inclined seats formed the sides and the open lake the background.

SITE OF THE MONUMENT.

The spot which is henceforth to be sacred as the last resting-place of Stephen A. Douglas, is situated four miles south of the City Hall of Chicago, and in plain view from that building. The grounds were recently purchased from the late widow of Mr. Douglas, by the State of Illinois, at a cost of $25,000. The monument is surrounded by a beautiful grove of oaks, trees which in their nature better than any others typify the sturdy character of him whose grave they shadow. The grove is washed at its eastern edge by the waters of the lake, which, as they ripple on the beach, will murmur an eternal requiem for the dead.

THE MONUMENT.

The design of the monumental tomb of Stephen A. Douglas contemplates a structure worthy the character of the statesman, and creditable to American art. In describing its character and what its appearance will be when completed, we will begin at the foundation and trace its proportions as they have already been, or soon will be, erected by the builders. On a deep and firm foundation, prepared with the utmost care, there has been placed a circular platform or base, fifty feet and six inches in diameter, and four and a half feet in height, the outer circle of which consists of four steps. Upon this has been placed another platform of less diameter, but of the same height, with concave sides, and ascended by flights of three steps. It is on this broad platform, nine feet from the surrounding level of the land, that the sephulchre containing the sarcophagus is to rest. The sephulchre, when completed, will be nineteen feet square and eleven feet high, having its walls four and a half feet thick. Projecting from the four corners are four pedestals connected by massive archways. The chamber within will be ten feet square, and have an arched ceiling. The floor, which is level with the top of the platform, will be laid in mosaic or tile work. In the center of this chamber, visible to all, yet protected from vandalism by grated bronze doors, will stand the white marble sarcophagus in which is to repose the dust of the good knight who, living, did valiant battle in behalf of the people he loved. Close-fitting doors are designed to protect the spot from the inclemencies of the winter season. On the four pedestals already alluded to, projecting from the corners of the sepulchre, are to be symbolical statues in a sitting posture and of life-size. These are to be cut from light-colored marble or cast in bronze, and will symbolize the following ideas:—Illinois, holding in her hand a medallion of her son, illustrious, though dead, while by her side rests a sheaf of wheat, emblematic of her agricultural wealth, and the State arms, emblematic of her sovereignty; America, with a shield; History, with her recording tablet, and Fame, with her trumpet and wreath. Above the tomb, and supported by its walls, is the pedestal of the column. The four sides of the pedestal will be adorned with bas-reliefs symbolizing the advance of civilization in the West. First, a representation of the wilderness, with a wigwam and Indians hunting; next, the pioneer's cabin and men felling trees and plowing the soil; then a ship, representing commerce, and a locomotive and telegraph representing science, with a figure standing by piled-up bales and boxes and holding the caduceus, emblem of peace and prosperity; last, a schoolmaster with a group of children, symbolizing education, with a church and the capital buildings in the distance. The pedestal will also be ornamented with books, scrolls, flambeau wreaths and festoons of flowers. From this pedestal will rise the tall and graceful column, forty feet long, five feet and a half in diameter at the base, and three and a half feet in diameter at the top. The column is in six sections, and between the sections stars in bas-relief will indicate the States of the Union. A cap and sphere—together six feet high—will form the capital of the column, and also serve as the base for the colossal bronze statue of Douglas, twelve feet high, which crowns the whole, at an elevation of one hundred feet from the ground. The patriot statesman is to be represented in an erect posture, his right hand resting on the fasces, in illustration of his firm reliance in the Union of the States, and holding in his left hand a scroll copy of the Constitution, which was the guide of his public life.

The foundation, the base platforms, and about half the work on the sepulchre are completed, and it is expected that the remains of Douglas will be deposited in the sarcophagus of the monument sometime in October. The estimated cost of the entire structure is $80,000.

The material used for the base and sepulchre is what is known in Chicago as Athens marble, a fine light-buff colored limestone, quarried at Athens, in the vicinity.

THE APPROPRIATENESS OF THE DESIGN

of this monumental tomb to the topography of the surrounding country is worthy of remark. The exquisite adaptation of art to nature is one of the charms of what we admire in the ancients, and an essential feature of every work which we can, with any justice, term classical. On low, level lands like our Western prairies, those who have earned the right to be deemed masters of all who come after them, were accustomed to erect lofty structures, that could not be easily obscured, but would tower aloft as landmarks, attracting from afar the traveler's attention to famous and consecrated localities. The Egyptian pyramid and obelisk are examples of this. In Greece, on the other hand, where it was possible to fix upon a situation in itself commanding, the architect's labor was not to attain a lofty height of structure, but a solid and enduring building to mark the spot. Hence the prevalence of low but broad and spacious temples—built in the most substantial manner. The architect of the Douglas Monument has therefore followed in his design the best examples of art in this particular. It is but just that this sketch of the Douglas Monument should be accompanied with a sketch of

LEONARD W. VOLK, THE ARTIST.

Mr. Volk was born in Wellstown, Hamilton county, N. Y., November 7, 1828, and is descended from some of the earliest settlers of that State. His father was by trade a marble cutter, and several brothers have followed the same calling with success. His father finished one of the ten marble Corinthian capitals supporting the dome of the New York City Hall. Until twenty-one years old, Mr. Volk passed most of his time among the marble quarries and works in Western Massachusetts and New York. In 1849 or 1850, he first attempted modelling at St. Louis and copied, in marble, a bust of Henry Clay, supposed to be the first work of the kind executed west of the Mississippi. But this branch of his art did not meet with much encouragement in that new country, so that his trade was his chief reliance for support. He married a cousin of Judge Douglas, and on an occasion of a cousinly visit by the Judge, when he (Mr. Volk) was living at Galena, Illinois, in 1852, he was strongly urged by Mr. Douglas to remove to Chicago. This advice he did not heed, but returned to St. Louis, afterward moving to Rock Island, Illinois, where he engaged in the marble business in company with a brother. Again, in 1855, he was visited by his distinguished cousin, who, after the first greeting, said to him:—"I have come to repeat an offer which I requested your brother to make for me a year since. That if you desire to go to Italy, and study the art of sculpture, I shall be happy to furnish you with the necessary means to do so. I don't ask you to take it as a gift, but as a loan, to be paid when you are able; but never give yourself any concern about it."

This kindness occasioned the utmost joy to the struggling artist, and in the autumn of that same year he arrived in Rome. After two years of earnest study in that city and in Florence he returned to his native land, and settled in Chicago. His first work was the modeling of a bust of his patron, for which Douglas gave him many sittings, and in 1858—during the celebrated canvass between Douglas and Lincoln—he modeled a full-length statue of the former. In 1860 he modeled a bust of Lincoln. All of those works he has since chiselled in marble. The Douglas monument has been a labor of love and gratitude. Mr. Volk, while superintending its erection, resides in the old Douglas cottage, situated hard by.

THE DECORATIONS.

At each corner of the grave was erected a pillar about thirty feet in height. From these uprights spring four arches, draped with black and white, and festooned with roses. Round the base of the pillars were arranged a number of flags, and all the way up they were drapped with black and white, and with wreaths of roses and flags. The grave was covered with natural flowers. In front of the grave was placed upon a pedestal Volk's splendid marble bust of Douglas, and a model of the monument. No other decorations of any kind were on the ground.

The documents to be deposited under the corner-stone for preservation are: Records of the Douglas Monument Association; certified charter of the Douglas Monument Association; a copper plate with the names of trustees engraved thereon; pamphlet, by-laws, constitution and appeal; diploma of membership, blank circulars, agents' credentials, etc., of the association; medallions of Douglas, with the date of the laying of the stone; photograph of the monument; likeness of Douglas on porcelain, together with a photograph; Sheahan's Life of Douglas to 1858; last speeches of the great statesman before the Illinois Legislature and in the Wigwam; his funeral ceremonies in 1861; obituary addresses in the Senate and House of Representatives; eulogy before the University; miscellaneous documents relating to Douglas; United States medals and coins—gold, silver, and copper; specimens of paper money; copy of Douglas' deed of land to the University of Chicago; copy of each of the daily city papers; copy of *Harper's Weekly*, with the monument illustrated; first and last copies of the catalogue of the University; Douglas' ancestral record; statistics of the Chamber of Commerce of Chicago; first and last directories of Chicago; copies of the catalogues of the art exhibitions in Chicago in 1859, 1863 and 1866; charter of the Chicago Historical Society, and an autograph letter of the deceased.

THE ENTRY OF THE PROCESSION

was the first impressive point in the proceedings. A band of music preceded the *cortege*, a battalion of Knights Templar succeeded, and the representatives of the Masonic fraternity followed. The latter ascended the stand and rested immediately around the base of the monument, where they prepared to perform the ancient rites.

THE CROWD UNRULY.

At this point, just before the appearance of the President, the vast crowd broke the ropes placed around the reserved grounds and rushed to nearly all parts of the field. Order was fully restored by the exertions of the Templars and Ellsworth Zouaves.

THE PRESIDENT AND PARTY,

with heads uncovered, now entered the grounds. The order of their progress on foot was particularly noticeable. Seward had the President's arm, Welles and Randall walked together, Grant accompanied Romero.

HUZZAS FOR THE PRESIDENT.

At the approach of the procession the audience, as if actuated by one simultaneous impulse, rose to their feet. From the housetops, where the cars stopped on the shores of the lake, from the people in windows, in vehicles and even in the trees, one long and hearty huzza ascended. The demonstration betokened considerable feeling, being at once an indication of enthusiasm at the presence of the distinguished guests and an appreciation of the solemnity of the occasion.

A GRAND ASSEMBLAGE.

On the lofty platform, elevated above the rest of the assemblage, was seated the most important concourse that perhaps ever collected under similar circumstances. Most of the great officials in every department of the government surrounded the President. The youthful sons of Mr. Douglas were present and touchingly reminded every one of the sad object that had assembled the pilgrims.

CEREMONIES OF LAYING THE STONE.

The first in the course of the proceedings was a brief but appropriate address by Mayor Rice. The Masonic Grand Master of Illinois, J. R. Gavin, appeared in front of the stand and delivered a short, touching and eloquent address, in which he paid a glowing tribute to the memory of the illustrious deceased, both as a friend and as a Mason, and referred to the fact that a statue will be placed on the monument, visible to the voyager of this inland sea as long as starlight and sunbeams love to dance on its crested billows. The Grand Chaplain then invoked the Divine blessing upon the ceremony, when the ceremony of laying the corner stone took place according to the Masonic ritual. After blessing with corn, wine and oil the stone was lowered in its place, while minute guns were being fired, and the band played a dirge which seemed to solemnize all hearts.

NATURE ASSISTING IN THE CEREMONY.

Nature herself gave a character to, and as it were assisted at the scene. This was at the moment when the feelings of the assembled multitude were most intent upon the rites of which they were the spectators. The worshipful Grand Master of Knights Templar had poured corn and wine and oil upon the corner-stone; the architect had delivered to the Grand Master the implements of the craft of Masonary; the stone had been examined to see if the workmen had done their duty, and it had been pronounced true and square, and was being lowered into its place; the revenue cutter Andrew Johnson, lying close in shore; fired her first minute gun; the band of the Knights Templars in slow and solemn cadences, played Pleyel's march; the immense crowd stood uncovered, looking upward to the platform, all eyes moist and all hearts touched by the scene before them, when the heavens which had been for a time darkening, and sombre clouds had gathered over the grave of Douglas, dropped gentle tears of rain upon the sod underneath which lay Illinois' favorite son and statesman. Few were on the ground that lacked heart and sympathy, to contrast the smiling morn, when hurrying crowds and marshaling hosts and gay banners and pennants, and soul stirring music pervaded the streets of Chicago, and the cheers that greeted the long procession went up from ten thousand throats, with the solemn change that came over the face of the heavens and over the minds of the spectators at the moment when to the dull boom of minute guns and the solemn music of the band, large drops of rain fell upon their upturned faces. When the ceremony of the day was consummated and the corner stone of the Douglas monument was lowered into its place, the air again cleared, the clouds broke and the broad waters of Lake Michigan once more danced in the sunlight as the Grand Worshipful Master descended from his position, having declared that the corner-stone of the monument to the deceased brother had been laid with all the ceremonies pertaining to the Order of Free and Accepted Masons.

GENERAL DIX'S ORATION.

A PRAYER was then delivered by Rev. Wm. H. Milburn, of the Protestant Episcopal church, when the orator of the day, Major-General Dix, addressed the assemblage as follows:

FELLOW CITIZENS—The scene in which we are actors to-day, with all its surrounding circumstances and accompanying recollections, has no parallel in this or any other age. We are assembled within the confines of a city numbering over 200,000 inhabitants, distant 1,000 miles from the ocean, where thirty-four years ago nothing was seen but an unbroken expanse of prairie on the one side, and the outspread waters of Lake Michigan on the other—both extending far beyond the compass of the sight; nothing heard but the voice of the great inland sea from the sands on which its waves were breaking, or the more unwelcome voices of the savage tribes who roamed over these majestic plains, where, within half the span of an ordinary life there was one vast solitude,—all is full of activity and progress and the treasures of a polished civilization. Industry and the arts display their stores with a bounteousness which might well be mistaken for the accumulated surpluses of centuries; science is teaching the truths which have been developed by the researches of the past, and enlarging the boundaries of human knowledge by new discoveries; education is universally diffused; and, above all, the temples which religion has reared to the service of God, from every precinct and almost every street of the city point their spires to heaven, as it were in acknowledgment of the merciful protection under which it has triumphed over all the obstacles to its growth, and become strong and self-reliant and prosperous. Fellow citizens, in no other country of the present, in no age of the past, could such a miracle of civilization have been wrought. And now this great city and the great West, of which it is by comparison but an inconsiderable part, have poured out the tens of thousands who stand around me in a mass so extended that no human voice could reach your outer ranks. You have come here to render the homage of your respect to the memory of one who rose among you to the highest eminence for talent and for successful labor in your service. And the chief magistrate of the Union, who in the council chambers of the nation stood side by side with him in the darkest hour of its peril, and espoused with equal zeal and eloquence the cause of their common country when other men, with hearts less stout and faith less constant, quailed before the impending storm, has come to join with you in this act of posthumous honor to an honest, courageous and patriotic statesman, cut off in the fullness of his strength, his usefulness and his fame. Where or when has such a concurrence of circumstances existed to inspire one with great thoughts, and yet to make him, by their very greatness, despair of giving them appropriate utterance? No one need look out of his own breast for the impulse which has gathered so vast a multitude together—a multitude which no other sun shall ever see re-assembled. It is one of the strongest feelings of our nature to desire to perpetuate the memory of those who, from ties of blood, familiar associations or valuable services, have become dear to us, and by the will of God have been separated from us forever. There are thousands within the reach of my voice who have been made painfully conscious of this instinct by the bereavements which the unhappy domestic conflict just ended has visited upon them. When the burden of grief lies heavy on the heart, it is the first impulse of our nature to prolong the remembrance, to grave into the solid stone, which shall endure when we have perished, some appropriate thought, or, it may be the simple names of those we have loved and lost. Kindred to these tributes of affection is the debt of gratitude which a whole community, represented here in countless numbers, has assembled to discharge by the erection of a monument suited in its proportions to the great qualities of him whom it is to commemorate—to lay the foundation of the structure, which is to be piled up, stone upon stone, from the earth beneath our feet to the sky above us, and thus to symbolize the eminence to which he rose by his genius and his transcendent public services above the plane of elevation where the great mass of his contemporaries stood and toiled and struggled in the hard battle of life.

Thirty-three years ago, the year after Chicago was founded, a crowd of people were assembled at Winchester, in Scott county, in this State, to attend a sale of valuable property. When it was about to commence a clerk was wanted to keep the accounts, and no one could be found who was willing to undertake the service. At this moment a youth, slender in person and feeble in health, who had come on foot from a neighboring town, joined the assembled crowd. He was at once singled out by the salesman as one competent to the service, and at his urgent solicitation, and tempted, no doubt, by the offer of $2 a day, the youthful stranger accepted it. The sale occupid three days, and before it was ended he had won all hearts by his intelligence, his promptitude, his frankness and his urbanity. It was the general judgment that a young man of so much promise should not be permitted to leave the neighborhood. A school was provided for him; and thus as a clerk and a teacher, a stranger, without friends and without means, not twenty-one years of age, relying on the talents God had given him, on an industry which never wearied, and a courage which never wavered, Stephen Arnold Douglas entered upon the great field of his labor in the West. It cannot be doubted that among a people battling with the hardships of a new country the favorable impression which his first appearance had made was confirmed by a knowledge of the difficulties he had overcome in preparing himself for active life. There was no romance in his early years. His youth was the history of hard work and of a perpetual struggle to cultivate the talents of which he must have become conscious in his boyhood. He was born in Brandon, Vt., on the 23d of April, 1813. On the first of July ensuing, his father died suddenly while holding his infant son in his arms. The first fifteen years of his life were passed on a farm, with such advantages of instruction as the district school afforded. Having no other means of education, he apprenticed himself to a carpenter and worked two years at his trade, but was compelled to abandon it for want of physical strength. He returned to his native town, entered an academy and devoted himself to classical studies for a year. He then removed to Canandaigua, in New York, and remained there three years, continuing his classical studies and for a portion of the time studying law. In all these phases of his youth he evinced the same intelligence and the same energy which distinguished his later years. As an apprentice to a carpenter he displayed a remarkable genius for mechanics, and had not nature marked him out for eminence in another sphere of action, he might have become one of the distinguished architects of the country. In his classical and legal studies he exhibited the same capacity for distinction, and while engaged in the study of the law he completed, to use the language of his biographer, "nearly the entire collegiate course in most of the various branches required of a graduate in our best universities. He is next seen as a clerk in a lawyer's office in Cleveland, Ohio; then traveling in the West in pursuit of employment, stopping at Cincinnati, Louisville, St. Louis and Jacksonville, and at last making his appearance at Winchester, and commencing in the manner already described his great career of usefulness and distinction."

There is nothing more touching than his brief address to the people of Winchester, when he visited that place in 1858, after having become distinguished in the councils of the nation. "Twenty-five years ago," he said, "I entered this town on foot, with my coat upon my arm, without an acquaintance within a thousand miles, and without knowing where I could get money to pay a week's board. Here I made the first six dollars I ever earned in my life, and obtained the first regular occupation that I ever pursued. For the first time in my life I felt that the responsibilities of manhood were upon me, although I was under age, for I had none to advise with and knew none upon whom I had a right to call for assistance or friendship." Fellow citizens, the history of Mr. Douglas would not have been congruous, and it might have been far less distinguished, but for the hard struggles of his youth —but for his severe discipline in cultivating the intellectual powers with which nature had endowed him. We do not consider, when we commiserate the trials of the young and unfriended, toiling on their weary way to reputation and fortune, that it is this very process by which men are made successful and great. Spare, then, your sympathy for those who in their youth are contending with difficulties, and bestow it on those who, with all their needs supplied, and without the stimulant of want, are in danger of sinking into inaction and mediocrity. It is Providence which in its mercy throws obstacles in the path of him whom it marks out for eminence, that he may gain strength and courage and resolution in overcoming them. It is thus that the path to greatness is made smooth in after life by the hard trials of our early years. At the end of three months Mr. Douglas gave up his school at Winchester, and commenced the practice of the law in Jacksonville. A mere youth himself, he had already given evidence of his fitness to be a teacher of men. From this moment he became conspicuous throughout the State, and he achieved a series of triumphs unexampled in the career of any one of his age. At the bar and in the political field he took from the outset a leading part, meeting the ablest and most experienced advocates and orators in debate, and always coming out of the intellectual combats in which he was engaged with increasing reputation. Offices poured in upon him in rapid succession.

Early in 1835, fourteen months after his appearance at Winchester, he was chosen, by the Legislature of the State, Attorney for the Judicial District; in 1836 he was elected a member of the Legislature; in 1837 he was appointed Register of the Land Office under the Federal Government, and in 1841 he was chosen a Judge of the Supreme Court of the State. It is not possible within the limits of an address to say more than this: that in every position to which he was called he maintained the same high standing for integrity, talent and courage, and that with every advance in the importance of the offices he filled, he developed a corresponding power and capacity for the discharge of their duties. In 1843 he was elected a Representative in Congress, and from this period his reputation ceased to be local and became identified with the history of the country. His first effort as a speaker in the Federal Legislature was as effective as his first appearance at Winchester. A bill was before the House of Representatives remitting the fine imposed on General Jackson by the Judge of the New Orleans district after the receipt of the intelligence of peace between the United States and Great Britian, in February, 1815. During the siege the General had declared martial law and resisted the execution of a writ of habeas corpus issued by the judge. As soon as peace was proclaimed he rescinded the order declaring martial law, surrendered himself to the court and was fined $1,000. The bill before Congress provided for refunding the fine. It had been advocated chiefly on the score of General Jackson's great services to the country; and it was conceded that he had exercised an arbitrary power unwarranted by the Constitution. Mr. Douglas took different and higher ground. He contended that the judge was wrong in imposing the fine, and that the General did not "assume to himself any authority which was not fully warranted by his position, his duty and the unavoidable necessity of the case."

These positions were maintained with an ability so marked as to attract and command general attention; and from that time forth he was ranked with the ablest debaters, in a body numbering among its members some of the most distinguished men in the country. It was natural that Mr. Douglas, trained as his mind had been from its earliest years to habits of self-reliance, should, in dealing with constitutional questions, strike out from the beaten track of interpretation into new paths. The instance I have cited is not the only one. In a speech in the House of Representatives on the annexation of Texas, he took the ground that the right to acquire territory, one of the most vexed questions of constitutional authority, was included within the power to admit new States into the Union. So, at a subsequent period, as Chairman of the Committee on Territories in the Senate, he contended that the right to establish territorial governments, was also included in the power to admit new States. In nearly all preceding discussions, it had been assumed that the right to institute governments for the territories was included in the power "to dispose of and make all needful rules and regulations respecting the territory or other property belonging to the United States." The propositions thus advanced by Mr. Douglas, were stated and defended with his native clearness and force, and they may be considered as constituting an essential part of the great body of commentary by which the exercise of the powers referred to is surrounded, and in regard to which divisions of opinion will continue to exist, notwithstanding the practical interpretation they have received in the legislation of the country.

In 1846, three years after his election to the House of Representatives, he was chosen a member of the Senate of the United States, and he was continued in that body by successive re-elections until his death in June, 1861. As a member of both bodies he took part in the discussion of nearly every great question which arose during those eighteen years of unexampled agitation and excitement. His speeches on the annexation of Texas, the war with Mexico, our foreign policy, the aggressions of European states in America, the extension of our own territorial limits, the **compromise** acts of 1850, the Oregon, California, Kansas, Nebraska **and** Lecompton controversies, internal improvements, and **incidentally** the question of slavery, the prolific source of nearly all the agitations of the last quarter of a century, and of the civil war which has drenched the country in fraternal blood, are all marked by the clearness, vigor and boldness which were the chief characterist:cs of his oratory. It was perhaps in the patriotic but vain attempt to calm the prevailing excitement and close up forever the source of the dissensions which had so **long distracted** the country, by the preparation and defense of the compromise measures of 1850, that the great ability of Mr. Douglas was more signally displayed than in any other political labor of his life. In January, 1850, Mr. Clay introduced into the Senate a series of resolutions, hoping that they might be made a basis of legislation which would be satisfactory to the contending parties. While these resolutions were under consideration, Mr. Douglas, as chairman of the Committee on Territories, introduced two bills—one for the admission of **California** into the Union as a State, and the other for the organization of the Territories of Utah and New Mexico and the adjustment of **the** boundary question with Texas.

In April a committee of thirteen, with Mr. Clay at its head, was appointed, and all propositions concerning the slavery question were referred to it. On the 8th of May, Mr. Clay reported **from** the committee Mr. Douglas' two bills combined **in** one, with **a** single amendment. When introduced by the latter they provided that the power of the Territorial Legislature should embrace all subjects of legislation consistent with the Constitution. As reported by Mr. Clay, the slavery question was expressly excepted from the power of legislation. This exception was subsequently rescinded, and the bill was passed as originally reported by Mr. Douglas. The compromise measures, so far as they related to the organization of the Territories, were his work and they were founded on the principle that the people of the Territories, through their legislatures, should determine the slavery question for themselves "and have the same power over it as over all other matters affecting their internal policy." These measures, as you all know, though they were, at the Presidential election of 1852, approved by both the the great political parties, were far from calming the popular excitement. And when Mr. Douglas, in 1858, as Chairman of the Committee on Territories, introduced the Kansas-Nebraska Bill, it led to a fierce and protracted discussion. The object, as the committee declared in a special report accompanying it, was "to organize all Territories in the future upon the principles of the compromise measures of 1850;" and "that these measures were intended to have a much broader and enduring effect than merely to adjust the disputed question growing out of the acquisition of Mexican territory, by prescribing certain fundamental principles, which, while they adjusted the existing difficulties, would prescribe rules of action in all future time, when new Territories were to be organized or new States to be admitted into the Union. That the principle upon which the Territories of 1850 were organized was, that the slavery question should be banished from the halls of Congress and the political arena, and referred to the Territories and States which were immediately interested in the question, and alone responsible for its existence," and the report concluded by saying that "the bill reported by the committee proposed to carry into effect these principles in the precise language of the compromise measures of 1850." The repeal of the Missouri compromise was incorporated into the bill at a subsequent period as an amendment, and in this form it passed both houses of Congress and became a law in 1854.

Whatever differences of opinion may exist, or may heretofore have existed, in regard to these measures, no one at this day will call in question the patriotic motive by which Mr. Douglas was actuated, his deep anxiety to preserve the harmony of the Union, his sincerity and the great intellectual power with which he maintained every position he took. No opposition in or out of the Senate, no popular clamor, no fear of personal consequences, disturbed his equanimity or his courage. He threw himself into every arena in which he was assailed, and defended himself with an intrepidity and a manly frankness which always commanded the respect of those who differed with him, and with a vigor which often won them over to his own convictions. At no period of his life, perhaps, did Mr. Douglas appear so remarkable as on an occasion which you all remember—when he returned to this city in 1854 where he had often been received with triumphant demonstrations of respect, and appointed a meeting in front of the North Market hall, to speak in defense of the Kansas-Nebraska Bill. It was a moment of the wildest excitement throughout the country. Kansas was rent by contending parties; associations had been organized and armed, North and South—the latter to force slavery into that territory, and the former to exclude it by force. Such was the popular indignation that it was determined Mr. Douglas should not be heard. For more than four hours he faced an angry and excited multitude, calm, undaunted, regardless of personal danger, attempting to speak in the intervals of popular clamor, and at last quietly retiring unheard, but not the less unconquered and unconquerable. Fellow-citizens, no man that ever lived could have confronted such a demonstration of popular disapproval if he had not felt that he had done right. Courage and a consciousness of wrong are never companions of each other; and it may be safely said that there is not one of those who was then arrayed against him that will not, now that excitement and passion have passed away, bear testimony to the sincerity of his convictions, and the moral grandeur with which he maintained and defended them. The peculiar constitution of our government and the character of our people have given an impulse to public speaking unknown to any other country. Oratory is of the natural growth of free institutions. There are no orators where there is no freedom of speech. They degenerated and disappeared in Greece after the era of Philip, and in Rome after the era of Augustus.

Suffrage and education being nearly universal with us, all have the desire and need to know whatever concerns the administration of public affairs. The communication of intelligence in regard to the designs and the policy of parties by the press is, to a great extent, *ex parte* and incomplete; and the defect has led to a practice peculiar to the United States, of holding assemblies of the people in which all unite for the purpose of discussing public questions, both sides being defended respectively, by speakers of opposite opinions. This practice is general in the Western and Southern States, but less so in the Middle and Eastern. It is to be regretted that it is not universal. Nothing can be more fair than such a comparison and criticism of measures and opinions. When misstatements may be instantly corrected, there is no temptation to make them, as there is in mere party meetings; and the facts of the case being undisputed, the influence of the speaker, apart from the merits of his cause, depends altogether on the power of his eloquence and the soundness of his logic. It has the advantage of carrying before the great tribunal of the people in every neighborhood (for there is scarcely a locality in which such meetings are not held) the issues to be tried; and thus before the right of suffrage is exercised every man is enabled to form an intelligent understanding of the duty he is to perform. It was in this field of public debate that Mr. Douglas' oratory was, to a great extent, found. His labors at various periods of his life in traversing the State for the purpose of addressing these assemblies of the people are almost incredible; and the influence he acquired is due in a great degree to the impression which he made on these occasions by his eloquence and his logical power.

The most memorable of these popular canvasses, and one which is not likely ever again to occur, was that of 1858, when **Mr. Lincoln** and Mr. Douglas, both candidates for the senate at the time, and for the presidency two years afterwards, traversed the State, speaking together at different places designated by previous appointment and published for the information of the people. The magnitude of the issues involved in the election of that year (far **more vital** to the peace and permanent interests of the country **than any one** at that time could have foreseen, although subse**quent events were even** then faintly foreshadowed), the great ability of the speakers, the confidence reposed in them by the political parties which they respectively represented, and the immense **mul**titudes that were drawn together to witness so extraordinary a contest, gave it an importance **which no** similar trial of intellectual power has ever attained. The relation in which they stood to each other and the whole country so soon afterwards, give it, now that their earthly labors are ended, a posthumous character of heroism surpassing that which it possessed at the time. They may be said with perfect truth to have been the nation's representatives and the exponents of its opinions. They were actors in a political drama as far transcending in grandeur all other popular canvasses, as an epic rises in dignity above a narrative of ordinary life. In April, 1861, when the first gun was fired upon Fort Sumter, Mr. Lincoln and Mr. Douglas were again together, the former as President, and the latter as a Senator of the United States, taking counsel in regard to the measures to be adopted to vindicate the insulted honor of the government, to uphold its violated authority, and to save the Union from forcible dismemberment. Mr. Douglas advised the most ample preparations and the most vigorous action. I have the highest authority for saying that he had the entire confidence of the President, and when they parted, Mr. Douglas set out on that last great service of traversing the free States, and rousing them by his resistless eloquence to the great duty of maintaining the Union unbroken against the gigantic treason by which its existence was threatened. And thus these two distinguished men, so recently opposed to each other, came together in friendly confidence under the impulse of an exalted patriotism, and an impending national peril, forgetting past differences, having no thought **of themselves,** and desirous only of knowing how each could do most for the common cause. It pleased God that both should perish in carrying out the great purposes of their hearts. Mr. Douglas died of a disease contracted in his herculean efforts in canvassing the North and West in support of the war. Mr. Lincoln died by a flagitious act of cowardice and crime on the very day when the old flag went up on the battlements of Fort Sumter, amid the shouts, the congratulations and the tears of the thousands who came together to witness this significant vindication of the national power. Happily the one was spared till he saw the people of the free States inspired with his own enthusiasm in the country's cause; the other, till he had made his name immortal by striking from the limbs of three million human beings the manacles of slavery, and seen the last hostile force surrendered to the armies of the Union.

Fellow citizens, there is a view of this sudden revolution in the **social** condition of the colored race, which ought never to be overlooked. The proclamation of Mr. Lincoln abolishing slavery was an act of war, and extended only to the States which had taken up arms against the government. It did not reach Maryland, Deleware, Kentucky or Tennessee, which remained true to their allegiance. Slavery still existed in those States; and for its final extinction, for the consummation of the great measure of manumission, for the obliteration of the only feature in our political constitution which has ever been regarded as inconsistant with its fundamental principles of freedom and equality, the country is indebted to the prestent Chief Magistrate of the Union. His personal influence with the South has achieved what no power of the government could have effected—the adoption by three-fourths of the states of the constitutional amendment declaring slavery forever abolished throughout the Union. The glory of President Lincoln is to have, by an act of his own will, emancipated all slaves within the reach of his legitimate power. The glory of

President Johnson is to have completed what the former left unfinished, and to have made the Constitution what eleven of the thirteen original parties to it desired to make it at its formation. Two of the slave states refused to concur in the great measure of 1865, and it will be recorded in our history as one of the marvels of the times that slavery was abolished in Kentucky and Deleware by the votes of South Carolina, Georgia, Mississippi and Alabama. Let the fact be proclaimed in honor of the last named states, and it need not be doubted that the time is near at hand when they will find, in high moral considerations, and an immeasurably increased prosperity, cause to congratulate themselves that their names are enrolled in the great army of emancipators throughout the civilized world. In the State of Illinois, there has been no great interest for a quarter of a century with which Mr. Douglas was not in some degree identified. His views were eminently conservative. He opposed all useless expenditures, all loose interpretations of organic or administrative laws, all attempts to evade obligations resting upon legitimate compacts; and yet he was always one of the foremost in advocating judicious internal improvements. He was particularly conspicuous for his persevering efforts to secure the grant of lands from the United States for the Illlinois Central Railroad, to which so much of the prosperity of the State is due. It is no injustice to the representatives in Congress from Illinois, to whose active and zealous co-operation with him that invaluable grant was obtained, to say that but for his determined opposition, it would have been made to a private company, and not, as he insisted it should be, to the State.

You all remember his earnest and long continued exertions, extending through a series of years, to procure the passage of a bill by Congress for the construction of the Pacific railroad, the most gigantic enterprise of this or any other age. He addressed public meetings and wrote papers to enforce upon the judgment of the country the necessity of executing a work which he regarded as destined to become one of the strongest bonds of Union between the States and the people on the two shores of this continent, and as essential to the full development of our internal resources and our commercial capacity. He did not live to see the great enterprise commenced. But, thanks to him and those who like him foresaw its importance without being appalled by its magnitude, it is now in a course of rapid execution. It was commenced a year ago; the track layers passed Fort Kearney on the 20th of last month; they are now more than 200 miles west of Omaha; they are more than half way across the Continent. On the 1st of April next, this city will reach, by one unbroken railway communication, into the heart of the great plains which stretch from the Rocky mountains eastward, and be within 200 miles of Denver, in Colorado. Of the 3,300 miles of railroad required in this parallel of latitude to cross the continent, only 1,300 will remain unfinished. There is every reason to believe, should no unforeseen event occur to retard it, that in five years from this time the work will be completed, the Atlantic and Pacific oceans and the population on their respective shores will be united by bonds of iron which no man can break, and a large portion of the trade with China will be turned from maratime into overland channels. The results to which this improvement must lead, no human sagacity can foresee, and no human calculation compute.

. In connection with this subject, let me recall to your remembrance the general gloom which overspread the country when the late civil war broke out. The stoutest hearts were not without their misgivings, and even those of us who never doubted the issue, and who were determined from the beginning to fight it out to the end, without regard to consequences, had our hours and days of the deepest anxiety. While calling out, like the psalmist, from the depths of our distress, "*De profundis*," the gates of our valleys and our everlasting hills were unlocked, as if in response to our cry, and treasures which had lain buried in the darkness of ages were poured out in boundless profusion, to sustain us under the enormous burdens cast upon us by the war. To these prolific fountains of wealth the Pacific railroad is to convey us on its way across the continent—to the Rocky Mountains, the Sierra Nevada, and the lower gold and silver bearing ranges. The auriferous mountains of Europe and Asia have been penetrated and ransacked for thousands of years for the precious metals they contain. Ours are, as yet, almost untouched, and there is every reason to believe—I had almost said to fear—that the treasures which are to be developed and distributed among us will exceed all that history has pictured of the riches of the great oriental empires. For let us bear in our remembrance that the administration of wealth by governments is always a source of corruption; that communities grow less scrupulous as they grow more rich; that simplicity of manners gives way to luxury and economy to extravagance; and that rivalry in industry is succeeded by that worst and most demoralizing of all competition—emulation in expenditure. Social evils of this sort may be endured and made comparatively innoxious so long as public legislation is pure. I say to you then, men of the West, look to the purity of your representatives in your State legislatures and in Congress. Let them be men of talent, if they are also men of integrity. But let them, first of all, be honest and incorruptible. It was the good fortune of Mr. Douglas to have borne his part in the national councils, when incorruptibility was deemed as essential in a public legislator as chastity in a woman, and to have gone through life, during the highest party excitement, without a stain on his reputation in his personal or public relations. Impure legislation was the evil for which, above all others, the founders of our government had the deepest concern.

Quod nostri timuere patres,

and it is on you, as voters, holding in your hands the power of selection, that the responsibility rests of maintaining the stability of the government by confiding its administration, and especially its legislative functions, to pure men. It has pleased the Sovereign Ruler of the Universe to strengthen and uphold us in the seasons of our adversity and peril. Let us implore Him not to leave us to ourselves in the more dangerous ordeal of our prosperity. The oratory of Mr. Douglas was marked by the same characteristics which distinguished him in all the actions of his life. It was bold, earnest, forcible and impressive. It is quite manifest that he never chose as a model any one of the great orators of his own time or of the past. It is equally certain that he bestowed little labor on ornament. He seems to have had a single object in the preparation of his speeches—to express his thoughts in the simplest and most forcible words, and to give to his hearers the clearest conception of his meaning ; and it was from the steady pursuit of this object that he acquired the extraordinary power which he possessed of moving other minds, by pouring into them the overpowering convictions of his own. He never turned out of the direct path of logical deduction to run after a rhetorical figure. He never impaired the force of a plain proposition by loading it with unnecessary words. His style was the growth of practice in speaking rather than study—a practice which began in his boyhood, and which, through his early appointment to offices requiring argument and debate, became a part of his daily life. It is doubtful whether any man of his age ever spoke so often in courts, legislative bodies and in popular assemblies. He may be said to have been eminently an orator of the people. His greatest power was, perhaps, in influencing the judgments and feelings of the masses. And yet, in the Senate Chamber, he was scarcely less distinguished. He was for years the associate in that arena of the first men of the Union, often their opponent in debate, and never coming out of the contest without honor. Indeed, as a ready and effective debater he had very few equals. His long and laborious training in the intellectual battlefields of the West, his clear mental conceptions, and the direct and forcible rendering of his thoughts gave him a power in extemporaneous discussions which few other men possessed. It is unnecessary to say to you, who knew him so well, that there were occasions when, under the influence of strong excitement, he rose to the very highest flights of oratory; when the passion by which he was moved, broke out into those pointed and epigramatic utterances which live for years after the lips of the speaker have been closed forever. Such an occasion occurred in the debate on the Mexican war, in the House of Representatives in 1846, when he was but thirty-three years of age. Some of the ablest and most prominent members of that body had denounced the war as "unholy, unrighteous and damnable," when Mr. Douglas turned upon them with the following outburst of fiery indignation:—"Sir, I tell these gentlemen it requires more charity than falls to the lot of frail man to believe that the expression of such sentiments is consistent with the sincerity of their professions—with patriotism, honor and duty to their country. Patriotism emanates from the heart, it fills the soul, inspires the whole man with a devotion to his country's cause and speaks and acts the same language.

"America wants no friends, acknowledges the fidelity of no citizen who, after war is declared, condemns the justice of her cause and sympathizes with the enemy; all such are traitors in their hearts, and it only remains for them to commit some overt act for which they may be dealt with according to their deserts." Though Mr. Douglas was always a member of the democratic party, he never considered himself bound by his associations to support measures which he believed wrong. His sense of right, his conscientious convictions of duty were with him obligations above all party ties. It was under this high feeling of honor and self-respect, and with an independence worthy of all praise, that he broke away from the political associations with which he had been all his life identified, and denounced, resisted and opposed with all the resistless energy of his character, and with all the earnestness of his eloquence, what he denominated the Lecompton fraud. There can be no higher evidence of his stern integrity than his course on this occasion; no better illustration of the truth that, though party ties may bind us on questions of mere expediency, no honest man will hesitate to break away from them when the alternative is to do, on a question of principle, what he feels to be wrong. The last public appearance of Mr. Douglas was on two occasions, one immediately succeeding the other. On his return to this State, after the attack on Fort Sumter, he addressed the members of the legislature at their request, denouncing the rebellion, urging the oblivion of all party differences, appealing to his political friends and opponents to unite in support of the government, and calling on the people to come in their strength to its rescue from the perils which surrounded it, and preserve the Union from being broken up by force of arms. In a speech to the people of Chicago, six days afterwards, the same earnest appeals were made to them to lay aside all considerations but that of preserving the government of their fathers. On this occasion he was received by all parties with demonstrations of respect, surpassing in enthusiasm, if possible, all others of the great ovations of his life. These speeches, though pregnant with the most determined spirit, and with an undoubting faith in the issue of the contest, were obviously make under great depression of feeling. He had been one of the most consistent, resolute and efficient defenders of the constitutional rights of the Southern States. He had done everything that justice and magnanimity dictated to sustain them. To the members of the legislature he said: "Whatever errors I have committed have been leaning too far to the Southern section of the Union against my own;" to the people of Chicago, that he had gone "to the utmost extremity of magnanimity and generosity," and that the return was "war upon the government." It was this sense of the inutility of his own personal sacrifices and labors, and the ungenerous return on the part of those for whom he and others acting with him had done so much, that embittered the last days of his life, and aggravated the disease under which he was laboring.

A vein of sadness runs through these two last speeches, and seems now, as we look back to the events speedily following them, a prefiguration of his approaching death. On these two intellectual efforts his reputation may well rest, as examples of the purest patriotism and of an undying faith in the ultimate triumph of the cause of the Union A few hundred yards west of us, shut out from our sight by an intervening grove, stands the Chicago University. In the magnitude of its extent, the massiveness of its architecture and its well-balanced proportions, it is not only an ornament to the city, but a living testimonial of the liberality with which private wealth has contributed to the cause of science. Two hundred students are receiving instruction within its walls from a learned and accomplished faculty, and from its noble observatory astronomy holds nightly consultations with the heavenly bodies. The ample grounds, in the center of which the institution stands, were the munificent gift of Mr. Douglas, whose name the main edifice bears. The instruction which in his youth he labored so hard to obtain, he wished to see fully extended to the young men of this city and State. And thus shall the two structures—that of which he was one of the enlightened and liberal founders, and this of which you have laid the foundation to-day—stand side by side, we trust for ages to come, as great landmarks of civilization, on the shore of Lake Michigan, where little more than a quarter of a century ago majestic nature from the beginning of time had not yet been roused from her silent and solitary sleep.

And now, fellow-citizens, our task is done; mine in this brief and imperfect delineation of the character and review of the services of Mr. Douglas, yours in laying deep in the solid earth the foundation of the structure which is to bear his name, and stand for centuries as a memorial to your children of one whose talents, political and personal integrity and devotion to the public welfare you would wish them to know and to emulate. In the changefulness of human things the time may come when the stone which is to surmount and crown it may be brought down to the level of that which is to be laid at its base to-day. For families and races, and communities and empires, must, in the future as in the past, run their course and perish. But great actions, great virtues and great thoughts, emanations and attributes of the spiritual life—types of the immortality which is to come—shall live on when all the monuments that men contrive and fashion and build up to perpetuate remembrances of themselves shall, like them, have crumbled into their primeval dust. One of the greatest poets of the Augustan era, nearly nineteen hundred years ago, boasted that his works should live as long as the priest with the silent virgin should ascend the capitolium. Of the millions of treasure lavished upon the decoration of the capitol no trace remains; its very site was long disputed, and priests and virgins, with the knowledge of the mysteries they celebrated, have been buried for more than a thousand years in the darkest oblivion. But the immortal verse, in all its purity and grace, still lives, and will make the name and genius of its author familiar until the records of human thoughts shall be obliterated and lost. Thus shall be the name of him whose memory you are honoring be as imperishable as the history of the State in whose service he lived and died; borne on his annals as one who was identified with its progress and improvements; who illustrated the policy and the social spirit of the great West; who gained strength and influence from its support and confidence, and who gloried in its energy and its unconquerable enterprise. He will be remembered above all for those heroic words, the last he ever uttered, worthy to be graven on stone and treasured to the end of time in all patriotic hearts—words which come to us, as we stand around his grave, with a solemnity and a pathos which no language can express. When his wife bent over him as his spirit was departing, and asked him if he had anything to say to his children; forgetting himself, his domestic ties, everything precious in life, from which he was about to be severed; thinking only of his country rent by civil strife, and overshadowed by impenetrable darkness, he replied, "Tell them to obey the laws, and support the Constitution of the Union."

The orator was frequently interrupted by applause.

GENERAL GRANT SURROUNDED AND ENGAGED—IN CONVERSATION.

During the delivery of General Dix's oration, General Grant quietly left the upper platform and took a seat on the lower and larger platform, where he sat for a time quietly indulging in a cigar. He was unattended by any of his usual suite, but of course he could not remain long unnoticed. His admirers on this occasion, were such as to completely exercise the General's proverbial reserve. He was at first taken by surprise, but it is evident that the General can talk to some purpose when he pleases. Three young graces, utter strangers to the General, opened their batteries upon him, and, after gaining a little ground, and engaging the General in a chat, the youngest and loveliest of them, raised herself to the seat on the General's left flank, while another perched herself upon his right, the third cutting off all retreat in front. The General met their sallies and replied to them good humoredly, and there is doubt but we might have given an account of what the General said and how he conducted himself in this emergency, but we feared a too near approach with book and pencil would have frightened off the spirited young ladies, and drawn upon us the frowns of the General. The scene was, however, enjoyed by many, and a number of committee men who broke in upon it and carried off the General to the little embowered cottage which Mr.

Douglas in his life-time made a temporary resting place **when he visited** the neighborhood, got but little praise for their intrusion.

THE PRESIDENT'S SPEECH.

WHEN General Dix had concluded, the President of the **United** States was called for. He appeared at the front of the **platform** and delivered the following brief address:

FELLOW CITIZENS:—I have traveled over eleven hundred miles, having been invited to attend the ceremony of laying the corner-**stone** of the monument to be erected, I will say, to my friend, personally and politically, that in accepting the invitation to be present on this occasion, it was for the purpose of bearing testimony on my high respect for **a man** who perished in the public service, **and one** whom I respected and loved. (Cheers.) I have no eulogy to pronounce; that has been done better than I could do it, and it will be handed down and placed in the possession of all who took an interest in the history and character of the distinguished individual who is now no more. (Applause.) Some men may wear the civic wreath which the nation weaves for those who serve **their country** in lofty positions, or they may be graced with laurels prepared for those who defend **her in the** hour of peril, and their names may be engraved upon the imperishable records of national glory. This column is reared in memory of the legislator and the representative man. A consciousness of duty performed was his remuneration while living, and his reward will be the inscription of his name high on the cenotaph erected by a grateful nation to commemorate the services of those who lived and toiled for the people and the Union of the States. (Immense applause.) Fellow citizens, I believe in my heart that if we could communicate with the dead, and cause them to know what was transpiring on earth—were it possible for Stephen A. Douglas to be disturbed from his slumbers, he would rise from his grave, shake off the habiliments of the tomb and proclaim, "The Constitution and the Union, they must be preserved." (Great applause.)

SECRETARY SEWARD'S SPEECH.

SECRETARY SEWARD then came forward, in response to repeated calls, and said:

Like the President, I am not here to make a speech. Less than on any other occasion could I consent to speak without consideration. It would be a disrespect to the great dead to offer a hurried and heedless tribute to the greatness and fame of Stephen A. Douglas. (Cheers.) You have just heard, as all the world knows, that Stephen A. Douglas was concerned many years in the great affairs of this nation at the capital. You are not ignorant that I have been concerned in the same way; for the last eleven years of his life that I was an associate in the Senate of Stephen A. Douglas. During the last six months of that period I was a fellow laborer on the same side, in supporting the same great cause; and I say that cause was the Union against the rebellion. All the previous portions of that time we were in a party sense adversaries. It is among the proudest of my personal recollections that, although we were enemies as the world understands it, political men arrayed against each other by partisan combinations for ten years, and were political friends and associates only for six months, yet, notwithstanding this, the widow, the children, the kindred, the friends and the party of Stephen A. Douglas paid me the extraordinary compliment of asking me to be the orator on the occasion for which we have assembled. It proved this, namely, that Stephen A. Douglas was a great and generous man. Had he not been, he could not have gone through ten years of opposition to me without leaving in my heart a pang or wound. It proved that I knew all the while that he was a patriot, and that he thought me to be one also. When they, broken down with grief for his loss—struck down as he was on the ramparts of his country's defence—came to me and begged to commit to me the care of his great name and memory, I was unable to accept the precious trust. I am glad now that I declined, because I rejoice that the task of his eulogist has been performed by one who throughout his whole life was united to him in the bonds of political as well as personal friendship, and who therefore could more justly appreciate his great merits, and who, having sympathized with him so deeply and so long, knew how his fame ought to be presented for the emulation of his countrymen. I am sure the oration just delivered will live in history and the affections of mankind long after you and I shall have perished, and even after this corner-stone shall be crumbled into dust. And what, fellow citizens, made a whole nation admire him during the last eventful years of his life? What is it that has made us unanimous in the homage now paid his memory? It was because, in the most fearful **crisis that ever overtook** our country, he rushed forward to the country's defense, and gave up his life in the effort to maintain and save the Union of these States (applause), and through it to preserve to posterity the blessings which, **by the** will of Providence, it was designed to confer. It shows one great **and** important truth from which men in every age should **take encouragement.** It is a mistake to suppose the greatest merit on earth is **to** found an empire or state—there is a great deal more merit in preserving it. The study I have been obliged to make of the affairs of nations has satisfied me that he who saves a falling state is greater than he who founds a state. (Great applause.) Therefore, I think that Stephen A. Douglas, with Abraham Lincoln, will live in the memory and homage of mankind equally with the Washingtons and Hamiltons of the revolutionary age. For myself, I could not ask higher commendation to the favor of mankind in future ages than this—when they shall mark and read the trials of this our beloved country under the administrations of Abraham Lincoln and Andrew Johnson—that they may find that with Abraham Lincoln and Stephen A. Douglas I was in true association, and with Ulysses S. Grant and David G. Farragut, and with all the great heroes and all the great statesmen who have given **to the** American people a new lease of life—a life that I feel able to defy faction, sedition and powerful enemies to destroy, either now or hereafter, for evermore.

Tremendous cheers greeted the utterance of these sentences.

GENERAL GRANT'S RECEPTION.

General Grant was next introduced and received the most tremendous greeting, as he has through all the places we have passed. Admiral Farragut was, as usual, warmly greeted. The other distinguished excursionists were introduced and applauded.

VISITING THE OPERA HOUSE.

The excursionists, with the exception of the President, visited the opera house to-night, and were escorted thither by the committee of reception. They were applauded by the audience as they entered. During the evening, General Grant was cheered, when he rose and said they could get nothing from him as agreeable as they got from the stage. Admiral Farragut responded to the cheers for him by saying that he and Gen. Grant had made a bargain to speak three minutes and a half, but as General Grant had engrossed nearly all the time there was nothing left for him to say. This produced much laughter.

Secretary Seward, in return for a similar compliment, rose and merely bowed his thanks; Secretary Welles and several army officers, following his example under like circumstances.

INJURIES RECEIVED BY THE PARTY.

Admiral Farragut has seriously injured his hands while getting in and out of the carriage; one is bandaged. General McCullum has injured a foot, and several others of the party were more or less injured by jams in crowds.

The gross receipts of the Douglas Monument Association, on the occasion of laying the corner-stone, were as follows:

For seats	$3,581.00
For committee badges	114.00
For opera house concert (about)	1,000.00
For medals, etc	454.20
For photographs, etc., at registry	20.35
From four contribution boxes in Tremont, Sherman and Briggs Houses, and at the Committee Rooms, from September 5 to September 9, inclusive	1.31
At registry on the grounds	2.55
Amount raised by the finance committee prior to the 6th instant, and as reported at last meeting	6,500.00
Total	$11,673.41

There is no report from the gentlemen having charge of refreshment stands. The supposition is that nothing in that direction has been made. As soon as the bills for expenses incurred have been rendered, and audited by the auditing committee, the public will be duly informed of the amount.

L. W. VOLK, Secretary.

CHICAGO, September 11, 1866.

[From the Chicago Evening Journal.]

A PLEASANT AFFAIR.—During the progress of the ceremonies on the occasion of the laying of the corner stone of the Douglas Monument, the cottage of L. W. Volk, Esq., situated near the monument grounds, was visited by many of the Presidential party, the Committee of Arrangements, and others, who enjoyed the refreshments so bountifully furnished by the host and hostess. Among the distinguished guests present were Generals Grant, Meade, Dix, Custer, Rousseau, Admiral Farragut, Postmaster General Randall, General Rawlins, General Steadman, Admiral Radford and General McCullum. After the prolonged march of four miles, occupying nearly three hours, the refreshments thus provided were very acceptable to the party. A number of toasts were proposed and responded to by the gentleman present. The tables were loaded wth good things, and excellent taste was displayed by Mrs. Volk in all the arrangements.

The amount of $6,500.00, reported as having been raised by the finance committee of the committee of arrangements for the purpose of defraying the expenses, was expended by that committee, and the association proper was drawn upon for $1,304.69 additional, to make up the deficit.

On June 3d, 1868, the anniversary of Mr. Douglas' death, his remains were taken from the ground and deposited in a sarcophagus, the marble of which came from his native county, Rutland, Vermont, and was placed in the center of the tomb. While being conveyed by the trustees from the grave, the Germania Maennerchor sang a beautiful hymn. An impressive prayer was made by the Rev. Dr. Haven, and for a day or two the public was allowed to view the face of the deceased senator through the glass cover of the casket. It appeared quite natural, being well preserved by the embalment, and presenting no appearance of decomposition. The students of the University of Chicago acted as a guard of honor around the casket, some time before it was carried to the tomb.

In January following, a memorial was drafted by the president of the association, Walter B. Scates, with a statement of its condition, asking for $50,000 to complete the monument, and was forwarded to the legislature.

The amount asked for was reduced to $25,000, and thus amended the bill passed the House of Representatives. But from some negligence it was not presented to the Senate before the adjournment, and therefore went by default.

MEETING OF THE BOARD OF TRUSTEES.

Parlor No. 10, Sherman House,
Wednesday, 7th December, 1870.

In response to a call from President W. B. Scates, a meeting of the Board of Trustees was held at 3 o'clock this P. M.

Present Messrs. Scates, Fuller, Volk, Goudy, Stearns, Burroughs, Wilson and Chandler: Mr. Scates occupying the chair.

It having been stated that the chief object of the meeting was to consider and determine upon the propriety of removing the monument to the grounds of the University of Chicago, and of using the value of the present site towards completing it, Mr. S. W. Fuller, after some preliminary discussion, offered the following resolution, which was upon consideration unanimously adopted.

"*Resolved*, That in the opinion of the directors of the Douglas Monument Association, if the widow and children of the late Stephen A. Douglas shall first consent thereto, it is best and expedient for this association to make application to the next legislature of the State of Illinois for leave to remove the remains of the late Judge Douglas from their present resting place, together with the monument now erected over them, to some suitable place within the grounds of the University near by, to be hereafter selected and agreed upon between this association and the trustees of said University, and for the sale of the land now belonging to the State of Illinois and occupied by this association for its corporate purposes, and the application of the proceeds of such sale, or as much as may be necessary to the cost of completing the monument according to the original design, and to apply the balance of the proceeds, if any, towards the maintenance and preservation of the monument, in such manner as shall be agreed upon by and between the State of Illinois, the trustees of the University and this association."

Letters having been received by the chairman from Messrs. Turner and Treat, who could not be present at this meeting, were read, favoring the object of this resolution; and as preliminary to the consummation of its object, Messrs. Burroughs,

Scates and Gage were, upon motion, appointed a committee to confer with and obtain the consent of the widow and children of the late Judge Douglas.

Upon motion of Dr. Burroughs, Mr. C. Beckwith was also added to this committee, and another committee, consisting of Messrs. Fuller and Goudy, was also, on motion to that effect, appointed to memorialize the legislature, **and to prepare** such act or acts as may be necessary for its action.

The secretary, Mr. L. W. Volk, then stated that **he was about** to start for Europe, and would probably be gone **two** years, and tendered his resignation as secretary and trustee of the association, with the request that he be relieved from further duty, **and** that a committee be appointed to examine and audit and report upon his accounts.

Whereupon the Board declined to accept **his resignation as** trustee, but, on motion of Dr. Burroughs, accepted his **resignation** as secretary, and on further motion, Messrs. D. A. **Gage** and **John B.** Turner were appointed to adjust and report upon his accounts.

On motion, the board then proceeded to fill the vacancy occasioned by the **resignation of Mr. V**olk, which resulted in the election of Joseph B. Chandler as secretary.

Mr. S. W. Fuller then submitted the following resolution, which was unanimously adopted:

Resolved, That we regret the intended journey of Mr. L. W. Volk, to Europe, makes it necessary in his opinion for him to resign the office of secretary of this Association; and in accepting his resignation, we tender him our thanks for the unremitting zeal, energy and fidelity with which he has discharged the duties of his office and labored to promote the objects and interests of the Association.

A vacancy existing in the Board, caused by the death of **Francis C.** Sherman, a ballot was taken, resulting in the **election of** W. F. Coolbaugh to fill the unexpired term of Mr. Sherman, ending January 30th, 1872.

No further business requiring attention, the board, on motion, adjourned till 2 P.M. of Saturday, the 24th inst.

Attest: Jos. B. CHANDLER, *Secretary*.

The following is Mrs. Williams' (formerly Mrs. Douglas) reply to the Committee appointed at the foregoing meeting:

To Messrs. Walter B. Scates and others:

Gentlemen: In reply to your letter dated Dec. 3, 1870, which I have this day (March 5, 1871) received through the Dead-Letter Office, I have the honor to say that I heartily agree with your Committee, and the Members of the Monument Association, in the propriety of removing the monument to the University grounds. It is my most earnest and heartfelt wish that it should be as speedily completed as possible, and I hope the legislature will consent to the sale of the ground and the appropriation of the funds to the immediate completion of the monument. My step-sons, Robert and Stephen, are of the same mind.

Your Committee's letter reached me without stamp, and simply addressed to Mrs. A. Williams, only after being opened at the Dead-Letter Office, after the lapse of three months. This will, I hope, excuse my apparent negligence of so important a subject. With respects, gentlemen, I am very truly yours.

Adele Williams.

Washington, D. C., March 5, 1871.

No definite action was taken by the trustees for the removal of the monument till 1875, and meanwhile, in 1873, another memorial to the legislature, asking for $50,000 to complete the monument where begun, was presented by a member of the House of Representatives from Chicago, Mr. W. H. Condon, who earnestly and efficiently labored for its passage, and was ably assisted by his colleagues Judge Bradwell, General Sherman and others; and just before the recess of the legislature the bill passed the House, with two votes to spare.

The following is the financial statement, as submitted to the legislature with the last memorial, dating from the organization of the society to January 1, 1871, and signed by the president and treasurer:

Amount by subscriptions in sums from $500 to $20	$ 2,856.40
From sales of photographs and engravings of Douglas and the monument, diplomas of membership, and small contributions	8,137.32
Sale of seats at laying of corner-stone	3,581.00
Sale of concert tickets, opera-house, on same occasion	1,006.08
Sale of donated real estate (2 lots, each 120x50 feet)	6,000.00
Total	$21,580.80

AMOUNTS PAID OUT:

Building foundations and first section of monument, marble sarcophagus, iron doors, fencing and grading............	$12,275.00
Expenses laying corner-stone, September 6, 1866............	1,304.69
Photographs, engravings, diplomas and medals............	2,227.08
Stationery and postage............	57.00
Agents' commissions............	506.68
Taxes on real estate............	157.15
Sidewalk and fence in front of monument grounds............	351.00
Design of Douglas monument............	75.00
Lithographing monument............	314.00
Printing diplomas, pamphlets, circulars, and office furniture............	962.32
Secretary's services, eight years, including office rent, furnished by him............	3,321.78
Balance in treasurer's hands............	29.10
Total............	$21,580.80

Several hundred dollars' worth of photographs, engravings, diplomas, steel-plates of diplomas, medals, and office furniture belonging to the association, were destroyed in the great fire, but its important books and papers **escaped**.

At the adjourned session held the following winter of 1874, the House bill came up in its order in the Senate, but was defeated.

DISPATCH FROM MR. CONDON.

SPRINGFIELD, Ill. Apl. 24, 1873.

To LEONARD W. VOLK, Chicago:

We have passed the bill only two votes to spare.

(Signed.)   WM. H. CONDON.

In 1875 the bill for removal of the monument was presented in the House of Representatives by authority of the Trustees.

A BILL

FOR AN ACT ENTITLED "AN ACT TO REMOVE AND COMPLETE THE DOUGLAS MONUMENT." INTRODUCED BY MR. HISE.

SECTION 1. Be it enacted by the People of the State of Illinois, represented in the General Assembly. That the "Douglas Monument Association" is hereby authorized and empowered to remove the "Douglas Monument," from the grounds upon which the same now stands, to such locality in the grounds of the University of Chicago as may be agreed upon between the board of trustees of the said university and the board of directors of the "Douglas

Monument Association." And power and authority is hereby given to the said board of trustees of the said University and the said board of directors of the "Douglas Monument Association" to agree upon such re-location of said monument within said grounds of the said University of Chicago, to preserve the ground upon which said monument shall be so re-built for the use of the same, and to fix and agree upon the terms for the maintenance, repair and custody of said monument and grounds.

§ 2. Said board of directors of the "Douglas Monument Association" are hereby authorized and empowered to make sale or sales of all that lot, piece or parcel of land, situate in the county of Cook and State of Illinois, whereon the Douglas Monument now stands, and known and described as follows, viz: lot one (1), in the lower tier of Oakenwald subdivision, fronting on Woodland Park and Douglas Place, of a part of the south half of the north-east quarter of section thirty-four, in township thirty-nine north, range fourteen east of the third principal meridian, in the city of Chicago, together with the appurtenances thereunto belonging, for such price and upon such terms as they may deem most advantageous; and the Governor of the State of Illinois, for the time being, be and he is hereby authorized and empowered to execute all necessary deeds of conveyance of said premises to carry into effect any sale or sales made by said board of directors, and any and all preliminary contracts to effectuate any sales that may be made by the said board of directors on credit: *Provided*, that said board of directors shall be entitled to no compensation for services rendered under the provisions of this act; *and provided further*, that no sale shall be made by said directors until the written consent of Mrs. **Adele Williams**, formerly Mrs. Senator Douglas, shall have first been obtained.

3d. Said board of directors of the Douglas Monument Association is hereby authorized and empowered to remove the said Douglas monument from the grounds whereon it now stands, and to re-erect and finish, and complete the same according to the plans and specifications adopted by the Douglas Monument Association, or such others as may be adopted, on such location as may be selected, as hereinbefore provided; and for that purpose they are hereby authorized and empowered to expend the proceeds of the sale of the grounds whereon said monument now stands, or so much thereof as may be necessary, for the completion of said monument according to said plans and specifications, and the protection and preservation of the ground upon which it may be erected.

4th. That if there shall be any balance left of the proceeds resulting from the sale of said lands after the completion of said monument, such balance shall be invested in United States bonds, or bonds of the State of Illinois, and the income to be derived therefrom, shall be applied toward the preservation and protection of said monument, and of the grounds immediately adjacent thereto.

About the same time the following bill for an appropriation to complete the monument where begun, was introduced in the Senate by Mr. Hodges.

A BILL

FOR AN ACT TO APPROPRIATE FIFTY THOUSAND DOLLARS TO COMPLETE THE DOUGLAS MONUMENT AT CHICAGO.

SECTION 1. Be it enacted by the people of the State of Illinois, represented in the **General** Assembly, that Walter B. Scates, Joseph B. Chandler, Joshua L. Marsh, J. H. McVicker, Melville W. Fuller and Potter Palmer, all **of the** city of Chicago, and Benjamin F. Fridley, of Kane county, Illinois, be and they are hereby constituted commissioners of the Douglas Monument at Chicago, and are empowered to receive proposals and contract for the completion of the Douglas Monument: *Provided*, that said commissioners shall not obligate the State of Illinois to exceed the **sum** named in section three of this act.

SEC. 2. Said commissioners shall receive no compensation for their services.

SEC. 3. **For the** purpose of defraying the cost of the completion of said monument, the sum of fifty thousand dollars is hereby appropriated out of the State treasury, and the auditor of public accounts is hereby authorized to draw his warrant on the State treasurer for said amount, out of money not otherwise appropriated, upon the certificate of a majority of the said commissioners, from time to time, as may be necessary, during the progress of the work: *Provided*, no money shall be drawn under the provisions of this act prior to the first day of April, A. D. 1876, which is made payable out of revenue from the assessments for the year A. D. 1875.

AMENDMENT.

Amend section 1, after the words " of Kane county, Illinois," by inserting the names of "William A. Richardson, of Adams county, Illinois, and Gustavus Koerner, of St. Clair county, Illinois."

Thereupon, Mr. Hise did not press the bill for removal, in the House, and after the passage of the Senate bill appropriating $50,000, he, with other members, labored to pass it in the House. But on the final vote the bill failed to pass, for the want of a constitutional majority—lacking some five votes.

[From the Illinois State Register.]

It is a pity the House refused to concur in the Senate's bill, appropriating $50,000 for the purpose of erecting a monument to the memory of the great Douglas. This it did this morning. Douglas' remains would not to-day be in Illinois soil, were it not for the fact that prominent citizens of the State, regardless of party, begged his widow to allow them to be interred here, at the time of his death. The House has struck an economical vein, but is very inconsistent. To-day, within one hour's time it refused to pay a debt of honor to the memory of a man who has done more for the state than any other man that ever belonged to Illinois, on the score of its "costing too much," and immediately, by a vote, continued the useless fraud-protecting and expensive election registry system, that costs the tax-payers of Illinois not less than *two hundred thousand dollars annually!* Next in order will be "Copperas creek," an unconstitutional taking of the people's money; and if our vote would pass this appropriation it would never be made.

At the next legislature, two years later, the same appropriation bill, except as to names of commissioners, was introduced in the house by Mr. Jos. E. Smith, member from Chicago, who worked untiringly for the measure, and had the satisfaction of seeing the following bill pass both houses and become a law.

A BILL

FOR AN ACT TO APPROPRIATE FIFTY THOUSAND DOLLARS TO COMPLETE THE DOUGLAS MONUMENT AT CHICAGO.

SECTION 1. Be it enacted by the people of the State of Illinois, represented in the General Assembly, that John D. Caton, Thomas

Drummond, Lyman Trumbull, Melville W. Fuller, Robert T. Lincoln and Potter Palmer, all of the city of Chicago, county of Cook, Benjamin F. Fidley, of Kane county, Gustavus Koerner, of St. Clair county, and Ralph Plumb, of LaSalle county, Illinois, be and they are hereby constituted commissioners of the Douglas Monument at Chicago, and are authorized and empowered to receive proposals and contract for the completion of the Douglas monument: *provided*, that said commissioners shall not obligate the State of Illinois to exceed the sum named in section three of this act.

Sec. 2. Said commissioners shall receive no compensation for their services.

Sec. 3. For the purpose of defraying the cost of the completion of said monument, the sum of fifty thousand dollars is hereby appropriated out of the State treasury, and the auditor of public accounts is hereby authorized to draw his warrant on the State treasury for said amount, out of the money not otherwise appropriated, upon the certificate of a majority of the said commissioners, from time to time during the progress of the work: *Provided*, no money shall be drawn under the provisions of this act prior to the first day of April, A. D. 1877, which is made payable out of revenue from the assessments for the year 1876.

[From the Chicago Times, March 24, 1877.]

THE ILLINOIS HOUSE PASSES THE APPROPRIATION FOR THE DOUGLAS MONUMENT.

In the house this morning, the special order being the discussion of the bill appropriating $50,000 for the completion of the Douglas Monument, Mr. Smith, who introduced the measure, made a strong speech in its favor. He said that justice and right demanded the passage of this bill. From time immemorial monuments had been erected by grateful people to their great and good men. The pyramids of Egypt were but tombs of kings, and the mausoleum but a monument from a widowed queen to her departed husband. But if monuments were erected to those who had contributed to the moral or historical wealth of a nation, how much more should they be erected to those who, in addition, had contributed to the material wealth of the State. The persistent efforts of Judge

Douglas from the time he entered Congress in 1843 till he succeeded in passing the law, were given to obtaining from the Congress of the United States the land-grant to the Illinois Central railroad. This grant enabled the company to build that road which opened up the heart of the state. It has poured into the coffers of this state in cash the the sum of nearly seven millions of dollars. Year by year hereafter it will continue to yield to the treasury its millions. But these cash payments represent not a tithe of the material wealth which has come to the state through this great enterprise. The cities and towns along its line have become populous and wealthy, and lands which could not be sold for anything, now yield from $20 to $30 an acre in taxes.

It was Douglas' wish that he be buried where he now lies. The state demanded it, and purchased the land where his unfinished monument now stands. Attempts are being made to remove it, but it should be finished where it now stands. The state bought the land that it might have the power to prevent what is now attempted. It cannot be said that economy demands its postponement, for the state has now nearly two millions balance in its treasury. The state can well afford to pay less than one mill on a dollar of what Douglas contributed to the coffers of the state.

Mr. Smith closed with a tribute to the character of Douglas, speaking of him as a representative man of the genius and character of the American people.

Mr. Herron argued that there could not be any objection to the passage of this bill, except on the question of economy. There have been millions expended in the construction of public institutions, which have been as bread cast upon the water. Civilization is more exacting now than it was a century ago. The old church was the monument of Christianity a hundred years ago, but to-day we do not hear the vials of wrath thundered from the pulpit. We hear that God and Christianity are realities. Monuments are erected to show the progress the human family are making in civilization. If this be true, it is meet that we should preserve the memory of him who has stamped his name as among the great of earth. Mr. Herron continued with a history of Douglas' record in this state, especially during the critical period when the state of South Carolina fired on the Star of the West and arrayed herself against the Federal Government.

Mr. Connelly—Did he sever his relations with the democratic party in the stand he then took?

Mr. Herron: He did not; but he told them there was no time to discuss party affiliations; the country was in danger, and the first duty of democrats was to rush into and close up the chasm; after that they could unite for political warfare. After the children of Israel crossed the Jordan, Joshua commanded each of the twelve tribes to take a stone and build therefrom a monument. He said to his people: "When your children shall ask their fathers, in time to come, 'What mean these stones?' then you shall let your children know, saying Israel came over this Jordan on dry land." When your children visit the tomb of Douglas, they will ask you, "What means this monument?" You shall tell them it is the earthly home of him who forgot position for patriotism, and who died, as he lived, for his country.

Mr. Merritt wished to say a few words. He was not much in favor of stone monuments, and was not enthusiastically in favor of the deceased Stephen. Douglas predicted that war was disunion and the destruction of constitutional liberty, and his predictions had been verified. In the face of his opinions he had joined with Lincoln in urging war, and with his skin full of brandy had pranced about in the vain idea that he was a second Napoleon. The speaker was opposed to the appropriation, on the grounds that enough money had already been subscribed for the purpose contemplated, expended and not been accounted for, and that his reputation was a part of history, more enduring than stone.

Morris, of Hardin, followed in a brief speech supporting the object of the bill, and was succeded by Morrison, of Christian, who denied in emphatic language that Merritt's speech represented the sentiment of the democratic party or the sentiment of a constituency Merritt had left in Marion. What has Douglas done? He united in contributing to the country's salvation at a time when such effort was vital. The gentleman from Marion had said if he had died before the delivery of his war speeches, he would have left a reputation more lasting than brass. True, but to-day there would have been no country in which to enjoy constitutional liberty.

Mr. James was in favor of commemorating the excellence of great men, but was apprehensive that the means suggested were illegal, and the end to be attained unnecessary. He did not need a monument, and he didn't think it was right to take money from the public treasury for the purposes suggested, and for those reasons he should vote against the measure. If, however, it was indispensable that his memory should be perpetuated, let it be done by voluntary contributions.

Rowett moved the previous question, but at the solicitation of many on the republican side of the house, who were solicitous lest there piece wouldn't be spoken, he withdrew the motion, and Dunne, of Cook, addressed the House in support of the bill. He said a great state should do honor to its illustrious dead. Therefore, Illinois should do honor to the memory of Douglas, and in no more fitting way can she do this than by erecting a suitable monument over his remains. Let no paltry consideration of expense defer this merited tribute any longer. Let no party prejudice hinder its accomplishment. Stephen A. Douglas spent his life in the service of the state, and died in his prime with his armor still on He died not alone in the service of Illinois, but although disease had stricken him, he hesitated not to raise his voice in an eloquent and patriotic appeal for his country, and died before its echoes had ceased to reverberate in the hearts of thousands of his fellows. With his death Illinois lost her most brilliant and illustrious statesman, the nation one of its most devoted champions. Lincoln and Douglas, patriots both, the sons of Illinois, died battling for the preservation of the Union, and their names will go down to posterity associated with the hallowed names of the fathers of the republic. The one sleeps the everlasting sleep of the just and good within sight of this hall, beneath the splendid obelisk erected over his remains by the patriotic and grateful people of the nation, in Oak Ridge cemetery; the other lies buried beneath an incompleted and crumbling tomb on the beautiful spot selected by himself on the shores of Lake Michigan, his coffin exposed to the vicissitudes of the weather, reminding the visitor forcibly and sadly of the old-time saying that republics are ungrateful.

The services of this great man, who, during his life, was the idol of his party and the admiration and pride of his country, are worthy of more honorable recognition, and no remains are deserving more decent sepulchre, and it is a burning shame and disgrace to the people of this great and rich state that he, on whose words thousands hung entranced as he uttered his last memorable sentences of patriotic fervor and devotion to the cause of free government in this land, should now lie uncared for and forgotten, with no fitting monument to tell the traveler who, with reverent steps, visits his grave, where his remains are laid. Gentlemen tell us that he needs no monument to recall his fame; that his great deeds, and particularly the great railroad that runs through the state, which he did so much to have constructed, is a more enduring and glorious monument than any he could erect. That may be true, but,

7

gentlemen, that was founded by him, not in his own honor, but for the prosperity and benefit of his people. It is our duty to manifest our respect and admiration for the great departed by at least erecting a memorial over his remains. I trust that no niggardly economy, nor partisan feeling, will defeat this appropriation, I know that our constituency will approve of our action, and that no legislative action we may take in this session will be more generally commended.

Mr. Phillips, of Montgomery, opposed the appropriation, and at the conclusion of his remarks the House took a recess until 2:30 P. M. When the house convened after recess, Mr. Winter, of Bloomington, led off in a brisk and fervent speech in favor of the measure. He claimed, that as $60,000 had been appropriated by the state for the building of a monument for Lincoln, it was no more than fair and just that $50,000 should be appropriated to the erection of a monument to perpetuate the memory of Douglas.

Mr. Rowett followed with a warm argument, also in favor of the appropriation. He believed it was a patriotic duty which this assembly owed to the people of the State and to the memory of a great man, to build a monument over his remains.

The roll was called, and when the name of Pinney was reached, he explained his vote by leave of the House. He believed the bill was for a patriotic purpose, and he should cast his vote for it. Mr. Matthews also explained his vote, during which he stated that he was in favor of the bill, and hoped enough of the republicans would change their votes to cause it to pass.

Mr. Wall thought that Mr. Merritt had insulted the young democracy of Illinois, in his remarks to the House, and he should therefore vote aye.

Mr. Chambers explained his vote by claiming that the people of the state should be consulted as to the time this expenditure should take place. He wanted to cast his vote for the bill.

Mr. Jack also voted aye.

The bill was passed by a vote of 81 to 40. The following is the vote:

YEAS—Abel, Allen, Bartholow, Bibb, Bielfeldt, Bower, Brown, Buckmaster, Busey, Byers, Callon, Chambers, Chesley, Clover, Cronkrite, Crooker, Davis, Dennis, Dunne, Easton, English, Evans of Kane, Foutch, Graham, Granger, Hall, Hendrickson, Herrington, Herron, Hickey, Hopkins, Irvin, Jack, Jay, Kearney, Kedzie, King, Kiolbassa, Leiper, Lott, Matthews, McCreery, Mitchell, Monohon, Mooneyham, Moore, Morris, Morrison of Christian, Morrison of Morgan, Neal, Oakwood, Palmer, Pinney, Raley, Reavill, Reed, Robison of Fulton, Rourke, Rowett, Secrist, Sexton, Sheridan, Sittig, Smith of Cook, Smith of Sangamon, Smith of Tazewell, Stowell, Taylor of Cook, Taylor of Kankakee,

Thomas, Thompson, Truesdel, Voss, Wall, Wentworth, Wilderman, Wilkinson, Winter, Wood, Woodward, Wright, Zepp, Mr. Speaker—82.

NAYS—Albright, Baldwin, Black, Boyd, Browning, Budlong, Collier, Connelly, Curtis, Evans of Bond, Fosbender, Fritts, Gill, Goodrich, Gray, Halley, Heslet, Hogge, Hollister, Hurd, James, Kouka, Latimer, Mace, Merritt, Nevitt, Pierce of Pope, Phillips of Franklin, Phillips of Montgomery, Ranney, Reaburn, Ross, Taggart, Tierney, Tyrrell, Vandeventer, Walker, Washburn, Wells, Whitaker of McDonough, Wilderman—41.

ABSENTEES—Armstrong, Ashton, Berry, Boydstone, Cannon, Duwey, Fountain, Fox, Gilbert, Grennell, Heffernan, Klehm, Koplin, Lindsey, McKindley of Madison, Powell, Powers, Ramsey, Reman, Robinson of Effingham, Roche, Rogers, Sherman, Tice, Watkins, Westfall, Wheeler, Whitaker of St. Clair, and Williams—30.

[From the Chicago Evening Journal.]

HON. JOSEPH E. SMITH'S ELOQUENT APPEAL IN BEHALF OF THE DOUGLAS MONUMENT.

DELIVERED IN THE ILLINOIS HOUSE OF REPRESENTATIVES, FRIDAY, MARCH 23.

Mr. Speaker:—I approach the consideration of this subject this morning in the earnest hope that, when the discussion is concluded, this bill, which is not now for the first time before the General Assembly of this State, may pass this House by a large majority, in which event I feel assured that it will also in due time pass the Senate, receive the Executive approval, and become a law.

It seems to me, Mr. Speaker, that justice and right alike require that this bill be passed; and my hope is that I may be able to convince at least a constitutional majority of this House that such is the fact, before I conclude the remarks, necessarily brief, that I shall make in its support; for if it be true that justice and right demand the passage of this bill, surely gentlemen will not hesitate to vote the appropriation, and especially will this be so when they take into consideration the other fact, sufficient, it would seem, in itself, that it is asked to complete a monument, now partially constructed, on land owned by the State, and designed to perpetuate the memory of certainly one of the two greatest men that the State of Illinois has thus far produced.

It has been almost from time immemorial, certainly so far back as history has left us a record, the uniform practice of nations and peoples to erect to their great and good men lasting monuments to commemorate their names and deeds. The pyramids of Egypt are but the monuments of mighty kings, and one of the seven wonders of the world was the mausoleum erected by a widowed queen to the memory of her royal husband. Indeed, sir, it will be found that all through the ages—barbaric as well as civilized—it has been the custom to erect monuments and monumental tombs, in some cases magnificent and costly, and in others crude and inexpensive, to perpetuate the memory of men who had done their State great service.

But, Mr. Speaker, while throughout all the ages monuments have been thus erected by grateful peoples in commemoration of the deeds of men mighty in war or renowned in peace, who had contributed to the moral or historical wealth of their country, where there is found an instance, like the one before us, of a citizen who in his life-time largely contributed not only to the honor, dignity and greatness of the Commonwealth, but also by persistent and determined and successful effort added immensely to the material wealth of his State; where you find a State that, like our own, has enjoyed for nearly a quarter of a century, is enjoying now, and for years to come—aye, for all time—shall continue to enjoy the fruits of the efforts of such a man,—it does seem, as I said before, that justice and right alike require that such services be commemorated in a fitting way, and that the General Assembly of a State like ours can well afford, and should not hesitate, to take from the wealth which such a man has poured into its treasury, enough to fittingly commemorate the great services he rendered to her. It will be my pleasure, before I conclude, to give some statistics showing in what the services to which I immediately refer consisted, and explaining why I claim so confidently that every principle of equity and fair-dealing demands that this act of tardy justice be done. Of course, sir, these statistics will show but meagerly the vast amount of wealth, which through the efforts of Judge Douglas have been poured into the treasury of the State. What we can touch and see can be approximately arrived at, but the remote and intangible cannot be calculated. I will, however, before entering upon that branch of the discussion, endeavor to give briefly the history of previous legislation touching this matter, and, so far as necessary, describe the present condition and needs of the Douglas monument and grounds.

Judge Douglas died in 1861, and in the General Assembly of 1865 a bill was introduced, which afterwards became a law, and is to be found in the session laws of that year, on page 18, appropriating $25,000 " for the purpose of purchasing," as the bill reads, " in the name of the State of Illinois, the lot of ground in which now repose the remains of Stephen A. Douglas, deceased." In that bill it is stated that this ground was owned by Mrs. Douglas. The bill further provides that "said land shall be held for a burial place for the deceased, *and for no other purpose.*" I hold in my hand that bill, which passed both houses, and was approved February 16, 1865. I also hold in my hand the original deed from Mrs. Adele Douglas to Richard J. Oglesby, Governor of the State of Illinois. It conveys the land mentioned in that act, is a general warranty deed, and states that "this deed is executed in conformity with the act of the legislature of the State of Illinois, authorizing the Governor of said State to purchase the premises therein described."

I am not aware that any measure has been introduced into this House or the other—but it has been mooted in the public papers —to change the location of this monument, and to remove the remains from the place where they now repose to some other locality in the city of Chicago. Douglas Park on the West side, the Chicago University grounds, the entrance to the Grand boulevard, and the entrance to Drexel boulevard have been mentioned, and some even desire—notably the Chicago *Tribune*—that the remains be removed to Graceland or Rosehill, and interred in one or the other of those public cemeteries. Now, sir, the act to which I have referred reads, "where now repose the remains." That plat of land which was purchased by the State for $25,000 was and is the place "where now repose the remains," and the sum so appropriated for its purchase is the only appropriation ever made by the State in aid of the Douglas monument. That land is worth now, even at the low prices of to-day at least double the amount that it cost in 1865.

In case of the removal of the remains by the State, the title would, in my judgment, revert to Mrs. Douglas, now Mrs. Williams; but whether this would be so or not, the idea of removal should not be entertained for a moment, and I am unwilling to believe that it will find a single advocate on the floor of this House. Besides, sir, it is a fact that the plat of land on which that unfinished monument now stands, was the only piece of land, unincumbered, which the widow of Stephen A. Douglas possessed at the time of his decease. It is unnecessary for me to state why it was that Judge Douglas, a few years before his death, became embarrassed and was obliged to mortgage his property, the principal part of which was finally lost. Had he been of a less generous disposition he might have died rich. But I do state it as a fact, and one which I wish to impress upon every member of this General Assembly, that it was the desire of Judge Douglas, frequently expressed, that his body might repose where it did repose at the time this bill for the purchase of the land became a law. That plat of land is on the borders of Lake Michigan; it is a part of that large tract which once belonged to Judge Douglas, and upon which he erected a cottage, and to which he gave the name of Cottage Grove, which it still retains. When he died there were but few residences erected in its immediate neighborhood, and it was his almost dying request that he be laid there, near the waters of Lake Michigan, and close upon its banks. He was laid there, and there he still reposes.

After his death it will be remembered that there was a struggle for the possession of his remains. Mrs. Douglas herself had expressed the wish that the body should be laid in the Congressional burying-ground at Washington, and but for the request of her husband, to which I just alluded, she would probably have insisted upon its being taken to the National Capital. But the State of Illinois persistently demanded that the body of her dead statesman should repose beneath her soil, and her persistency carried the point, and he was buried beneath her soil, on the very spot where the unfinished monument now stands. Sir, the State itself offered to buy this land. It was no request of Mrs. Douglas, or of the heirs, or of the people of Chicago, that this land be purchased by the State; but the State itself, of its own motion, offered to purchase of the widow of Stephen A. Douglas that lot of land which he himself had selected as his burial-place, and to pay for it its full value, in order that the remains might lie in the soil of this State, in land to which the State had the title, and so that no one thereafter could have the right, at any time, to remove those remains without the consent of the State and the widow and the heirs-at-law. Such is the fact so far as the purchase of the land is concerned. It was bought by the State at the request of the people; and it was then proposed to erect over the remains a monument which should be a fitting memorial of the illustrious dead. The State was not asked at that time to appropriate anything for this purpose, but subsequently a bill appropriating money to build a monument passed in one branch of the General Assembly, but failed to secure a constitutional majority in the other, and therefore did not become a law. Private subscriptions were then started, and other means resorted to to procure funds for the purpose, and upwards of $20,000 was collected, and so much of the monument as is now completed was thereupon erected. It has been stated, I am free to say, that in the payment of salaries, office rent, etc., several thousand dollars of the money so collected was diverted from the object for which it was contributed. On the other hand, it is asserted that every dollar was prudently expended. I prefer to believe and do believe the latter assertion. But be that as it may, the money, whether wisely expended or not, was all expended, and none of it remains. It served to construct so much of the monument as is now complete, that is, so far as to be fitted to receive the sarcophagus containing the remains.

This bill asks for an appropriation of $50,000 to complete the monument where it now stands. The high character of each of the commissioners named therein, is a sufficient guaranty that the money, if appropriated, will be wisely and economically expended; and I assure you, gentlemen, that with the amount named, the monument shall be completed on its present site, the grounds made worthy of the treasure they hold, and that no further or other sum will be asked by the Monument Association in aid of the one object or the other. Bills to accomplish the purpose sought to be accomplished by this bill, have from time to time been introduced into the General Assembly of the State, at one session passing one house and at another session the other house, but up to this time failing to pass both houses, and thereby becoming a law. In the meantime, the monument and grounds are neglected; cattle wander at will over the premises; the fences have gone to decay and fallen—only that of wooden pickets surrounding the monument itself remains standing—and within that narrow space the monument is cared for.

But, perhaps, gentlemen will say: "Why not erect monuments to other men? Is not this establishing a bad precedent? Shall we not be called upon by and by to make other appropriations of a similar character and for similar reasons? Is it prudent to do this thing?" These objections are not without weight. But, sir, I say to all who make them, "come and let us reason together." If we except that of Abraham Lincoln, is there now, or is there likely to be in our day and generation, an instance requiring at our hands the recognition that the one before us does? In view of the man and all that he did for us, do we ask anything that is not pre-eminently just and right?

I commenced, Mr. Speaker, by saying that to vote this appropriation was but an act of justice and right. Let me try to explain now why I so consider it. The older members of this House know, because they were here; the younger members know, because they have read and heard of it—of the long siege which finally resulted in the passage by the two houses of Congress of the bill for an act donating lands to the Illinois Central Railroad Company of this State. That act became a law in the year 1850. Judge Douglas entered the United States Senate in 1847; he entered the House of Representatives in 1843, being then but 30 years old. From the time he entered the House up to the time this bill finally became a law, he had devoted himself, all the while, with persistent effort, to obtaining this grant. True, he was not alone in this effort; the distinguished Justice Breese, who has for so many years adorned the Supreme bench of this State, was, during a large portion of that time, representing the State of Illinois in the Senate of the United States, and, as chairman of the Committee on Public Lands, devoted his time and attention and exerted his great influence and his every effort, while he remained in the Senate, to further the measure which Judge Douglas had introduced into the House, and subsequently so earnestly and successfully advocated in the Senate.

It was owing to the efforts of these two men that that measure was finally adopted. By the passage of that law, the Illinois Central Railroad Company received alternate sections of the public lands on the line of that railroad. Some question arose as to whether the road should be built on the line of the old Illinois Central road or follow a different course, and it is a part of the history of the State how that difficulty was finally settled by taking the old road-bed, and constructing a branch from Chicago, tapping the main line at Centralia. There was great opposition to this land grant in some parts of the State, because the proposed line of the road cut them off from its advantages. All these difficulties were finally adjusted by the construction of this branch line. Judge Douglas at the first feared that to include this branch line might result in the defeat of the whole bill, but was finally induced to advocate the measure, with the branch line included, and in 1850 the bill became a law. At that time the State of Illinois had a population of less than 800,000. Within five years its population had increased to nearly 1,500,000. That line of railroad which started over the prairie and through sparsely-settled villages, became alive with active, strong men and brave women, the founders of towns now populous and wealthy. The population of the State increased at an unprecedented rate, not only enabling the railroad company to build its road by the sale of its lands, and to pay the State, as it has done from that day to this, a vast income, but the General Government itself, which had donated this land found that by the settlement of the alternate sections still belonging to it, money was poured into its own coffers, so that the United States lost nothing by its gift, and the State gained and the road gained immensely. The Illinois Central Railroad was completed, an outlet for the products of the fertile Valley of the Mississippi was provided, and cities, towns and villages sprang up all along the line as if by enchantment.

The other day I asked the Auditor of Public Accounts, to have prepared for me a detailed statement of the annual receipts by the State from the Illinois Central Railroad Company, which, by the terms of its charter pays 7 per cent. of its gross earnings to the State. I now hold in my hand that statement. A copy has been furnished the press, and will be found printed in the morning papers of to-day. In 1855, the first year of its operation, there was but $29,751.59 paid into the treasury of the State. In 1876, the last year, $356,005.58. In 1865, the year of the close of the war, the amount was $496,489,84, being about $32,000 in excess of any other year; while the aggregate received into the State Treasury during the twenty-two years of its operation, from the Illinois Central Railroad Company, as shown by the subjoined statement, reaches the enormous sum of $6,976,607.48. The annual receipts have been as follows:

YEAR.	AMOUNT.	YEAR.	AMOUNT.
1855	$ 29,751 59	1866	$ 427,075.65
1856	77,631.66	1867	444,007.74
1857	145,646.84	1868	4 8,397.48
1858	132,005.53	1869	464,933.31
1859	132,104.46	1870	464,584.52
1860	177,557.22	1871	463,512.91
1861	177,257.81	1872	442,856.54
1862	212,174.00	1873	428.574.00
1863	300,394.58	1874	394,366 46
1864	405,514.04	1875	375,766.02
1865	496,489.84	1876	356,005.58
		Total	$6,976,697 48

But that amount, enormous as it is, represents only the cash that has been paid directly by the Illinois Central Railroad Company into the treasury of the State; it includes no portion of that added wealth of which I have heretofore spoken as incalculable, and for which the State is so largely indebted to the construction of that road.

I assume, sir, that no one on the floor of this House will deny that it was owing to the efforts of Judge Douglas that this sum was secured to the State. Without him the land grant bill would not have passed. Prior to its passage, Judge Breese, who had so ably advocated its passage, had retired from the Senate and been succeeded by General Shields, who also succeeded him as chairman of the Committee on Public Lands. But Judge Douglas, not leaving it when his associates left him, pushed the bill with renewed vigor and did not relax his efforts till it became a law; and I assert, Mr. Speaker, that but for his persistent efforts, this grant to the Illinois Central Railroad Company would not have been made and this road would not have been built, and this sum would not have been paid into the treasury of the State; and I repeat that vast as that sum is, it represents but a fraction of the wealth that this State has derived from the construction of that road. In popula- it has increased from less than a million to three millions and a half, and who can estimate the proportion of that increase justly to be credited to the building of that road, or tell in figures the value of that living wealth? Thousands of acres of land that a quarter of a century ago could not have been sold for a dollar an acre, are now yielding from twenty to thirty dollars an acre yearly in taxes. I do not say but that this population might have gone somewhere else in this State than along the line of that road or that other roads might not have been built; but it may be asserted without fear of contradiction that this great artery would not have been opened through the heart of the State, but for the grant which Judge Douglas procured from the United States of America.

Now what are the friends of this measure asking from the State? They are asking the comparatively small sum of $50,000. For what? It is not to erect a monument; not to start a new project: not to establish a precedent which may be bad; but they come before the General Assembly to say to us, the representatives of the great State of Illinois: "You have purchased and you own this plat of land on the shores of Lake Michigan; you purchased it for the purpose of depositing in it the remains of one of your greatest sons. Individuals have done what they could, and have left there a monument in an unfinished state, and we ask only that you take from the coffers of this State less than one cent on the dollar of the vast sum that Judge Douglas contributed to place in those coffers, for the purpose of completing this work, which has been so long begun, and which the State owes it to itself to finish." And speaking for myself, I say, Mr. Speaker, that it is a disgrace to the State that that monument should be left in the condition that it is now in, when comparatively so small a sum is required to complete it.

But it may be said that it is better not to do it now, as a matter of economy; that the State is called upon to appropriate large sums of money for charitable institutions, and that it is better to wait awhile. Anticipating this, I this morning asked the Auditor of Public Accounts to give me a statement showing the balance in the treasury on the first day of March, A. D. 1877. That balance was $1,771,309.17; our State debt is comparatively nothing; and I venture to say that there is not a State in the Union that can give a better showing. Of that money, during the last year, $356,005.58 was paid into the treasury by the Illinois Central Railroad Company.

Now, I rose, Mr. Speaker, simply for the purpose of giving these facts. I shall be followed by gentlemen who will give the record and illustrate the character of Stephen A. Douglas in more eloquent language than I could hope to do. I never in my life met him but once. I never heard from his lips but two words, and those were addressed to myself. Those words were "Get right!" But I must say that I knew him by his works. I knew him by hearing of him from those who were intimate with him, and who knew his worth and appreciated what he was. The true nobility and greatness of a nation consists in the nobility and greatness of its representative men. I regard Stephen A. Douglas as one of the two greatest men that Illinois has ever produced. I regard him as pre-eminently a self-made man. Coming into this State a stripling, with but two dollars in his pocket; serving as an auctioneer's clerk, and earning his first six dollars in that way; teaching school and eking out a meager livelihood till he attained his majority; stepping forth a marked man on the very threshold of his manhood, and going on "conquering and to conquer," I regard him as a representative man of the genius and character of the American people. I regard him as a man, honest, upright, just; of great power of intellect and of great strength of purpose; knowing and always pursuing the right; a man, in short, whom any State or people should delight to honor. And shall this State refuse to honor him—rather I should say to do him justice—when all we ask is that his unfinished monument on the banks of Lake Michigan may be completed? That on the foundation which the liberality of individuals has constructed, a column may rise bearing the statue of the illustrious statesman, and visible from the land and from the broad bosom of the lake, upon whose banks the dust of the honored dead reposes, a fitting memorial of the greatness of him whose achievements it is erected to commemorate, and of the gratitude of the State which honored itself in honoring him.

If, sir, my limited time permits me to allude to anything else which should operate to make men unite for the passage of this bill, let me briefly refer to those dark days of the Republic, when the black cloud of secession and disunion hung over this nation, and when we knew not whether out of that cloud should come the lightning stroke that would destroy us as a people, or whether from behind it the light of heaven should again shine forth, dispelling the darkness, and again illuminating everything with the brightness of its rays. Let me remind you, gentlemen, that in those dark days, Stephen A. Douglas rose up in his might, here in the city of Springfield, and in a speech glowing with eloquence and patriotism, put at rest all doubt, quieted all fear, and nerved the hearts of his countrymen to that mighty effort, the issue of which was the maintained integrity of the Union. Two months afterwards that voice, then so mighty for good, was hushed in the silence of death; a nation stood with bowed head, and the hearts of a great people were filled with a sadness inexpressible. Men who had opposed him in the political arena, and against whom the mighty power of his matchless eloquence had been brought to bear, stood sorrowful before the tremendous reality that one of earth's greatest men had fallen; while those who had been of his political household, who were his familiar friends, who had sat, as it were, at his feet, and drunk in the political wisdom that flowed from his lips, felt almost as if death had entered their own homes and taken from their family circle the form of a loved one. Like him whom Webster apostrophized so grandly, Douglas was cut off in the hour of overwhelming anxiety and thick gloom, and like his would I have the memory of Douglas endure, "wheresoever among men a heart shall be found that beats to the transports of patriotism and liberty." It may be, sir, that republics are ungrateful; it can never be that they are justly so. Carlyle has said that "the hands of forgotten brave men have made it a world for us." Forgotten brave men! True. But that such men have been forgotten, though it prove the truth not only of the adage that republics are ungrateful, but that all nations are alike so, proves none the less that they should not be.

Upon the one side of this house hangs the portrait of Abraham Lincoln, upon the other that of Stephen A. Douglas—Illinois' two greatest sons. In Oak Ridge Cemetery, almost within the shadow of the dome which rises above us, the massive monument to the former **towers to** Heaven, grand, perhaps, in its architectural design, grander **in its** purpose, grandest in that it is a memorial of the gratitude and **the grief of** a great State and nation. On the shores of Lake Michigan, within sound of the sighing of the waves of that mighty sea, unfinished and neglected, stand the foundation stones **of the** monument proposed to be **erected to the** memory of that other illustrious man, upon whom for **years every son** of Illinois looked with pride and affection. **The friends of this bill ask of** the State that honored Stephen A. **Douglas so much** while living, to no longer neglect to **do** justice to his memory. Let the monumental shaft at Oak Ridge Cemetery, and the beautiful **column on** the shores of Lake Michigan, as they point heavenward, **teach our** young men, as **they stand at the base** of the one **or the other, to** emulate the virtues **and the** example of those whose virtues and **patriotism those** monuments are erected to commemorate. **Victor Hugo has said** that it is well to celebrate the anniversaries of great events, for **such** celebrations stimulate to other great achievements. As truly **may it be said that** it is well to erect monuments to perpetuate the memory of the truly great, for they stand always as monitors, bidding the living strive to be also great, that their words and deeds may be alike remembered and honored by those whose **benefactors they may prove to be.**

In conclusion, I appeal **to** you, gentlemen, one and **all, to vote** the appropriation asked in this bill.

On the 15th day of May, 1877, **the** House bill was taken up by the Senate and passed without debate. It was approved on the 22d following by Governor Cullom, **and thus** became a law, taking effect July 1st, 1877.

The same Legislature voted an appropriation of **$27,000 to** complete the Lincoln monument at Springfield, and it was pre**sumed** that one measure assisted the other.

Pursuant to a call, the commissioners named in **the foregoing** bill **met at** the Palmer House **July 2d,** 1877, **and** organized, by the selection of a President and Secretary, and **an** Executive Committee.

The writer was requested to submit his designs for the monument, which were substantially the same as had been adopted by the Trustees in 1864—the original model of the design having been destroyed in the great fire of '71, he had since then reproduced it by drawings, with some slight modifications, and the same were exhibited before the Legislature of 1875.

These designs, together with plans for coping around base of monument, coping and sidewalk along Douglas avenue south of monument grounds, and a terrace wall along the railway track east of the grounds, were submitted and explained before the commission, and were unanimously re-adopted by the commissioners.

The next meeting of the commission was held July 7th. The *Chicago Times* of the 8th contained the following:

"The Douglas Monument Commission, consisting of Judges Drummond, Trumbull, Caton, and Fridley, and Messrs. Potter Palmer, M. W. Fuller, R. T. Lincoln, and Ralph Plumb, met in Judge Drummond's room, United States building, on yesterday afternoon, the full board present.

Mr. Lincoln, on behalf of the committee appointed at the meeting on Monday to make an examination of the design for the monument, as originally made by Leonard W. Volk, and in accordance with which the work was begun in 1868, reported that in their judgment it fulfilled the requirements in every respect, and recommended its adoption by the commission. The committee had taken the advice of a competent architect, whose opinion was that a granite shaft might safely be placed on the Lemont limestone base already erected; or, the monument could be completed with the same stone as that used in the tomb, though it would be necessary to see, first, that the foundations were well and carefully laid. The committee would recommend a division of the work, giving to Mr. Volk the statuary, and putting the masonry into the hands of an architect. In conclusion, the committee submitted a resolution to the effect that Mr. Volk be asked to submit double proposals for completing the monumental statuary; one stating time and terms for doing the work as a whole, the other, times and prices for the surmounting statue and the surrounding allegorical prices, separately, that the commission might choose.

Considerable discussion followed. Mr. Fuller favored a division of the work—one man to do the statuary, another the masonry. Judge Fridley thought the work could be done cheaper if let to one man, and it seemed to him that the most reliable person was Mr. Volk. Judge Caton was in favor of granite, and opposed to limestone for the shaft. So, also was Judge Drummond. He preferred advertising for the work as a whole. Mr. Palmer thought there should be an architect. The commission should advertise for proposals, and let each part of the work to the lowest bidder. Judge Caton suggested that they advertise for proposals both in whole and in part, and then they could choose. After some further talk the report of the committee was received, and the resolution adopted. On motion the same committee, consisting of Messrs. Fuller, Lincoln, and Palmer, was continued, with instructions to procure plans and specifications, and after a careful examination of them to advertise for proposals for the work, except the statuary. The commission then adjourned to meet two weeks from Tuesday next. The committee will meet at the Palmer house, at 2 o'clock this afternoon."

The following resolution was passed at this meeting:

Resolved, That the secretary of this commission be and he is hereby directed to request Mr. Leonard W. Volk to submit to this commission, at his earliest convenience, proposals for the execution and completion, including the placing of the same, of the statuary for the Douglas Monument, at Chicago, according to the design adopted by the Douglas Monument Association. Which proposals shall state the price at which, and the time within which he would contract to execute and complete said statuary in whole, and also the price and time for and within which he would contract to execute, complete and place: *First*, the statue designed to surmount said monument; *Second*, the figures at the corners, and *Third*, the Relief work; taken and considered separately.

A true copy of resolution adopted by commissioners to complete Douglas Monument at Chicago, July 7th, 1877.

M. W. FULLER,
Sec'y of said Commission.

At a subsequent meeting of the Executive Committee, held soon after, the writer was ordered to prepare working plans and specifications, to be made ready forthwith, for the superstructure of the monument, (i. e. **all that portion** above the tomb **to the base** of statue) **to be of a light-colored** New England **granite.**

Also, plans and specifications for coping around base of monument and along Douglas avenue, a sidewalk in **same** street, and a terrace wall along the railway.

The following agreement was made:

This memorandum of an agreement made at Chicago, **this first day** of August, A. D. 1877, between the Commissioners **of the** Douglas Monument at Chicago, and Leonard W. Volk, of the city of Chicago, county of Cook and State of Illinois, Witnesseth: That the said Leonard W. Volk, for the consideration hereinafter named, agrees that the designs, plans, drawings and specifications of the Douglas Monument at Chicago, already drawn and prepared by him and furnished to **said** Commissioners, shall and do belong to the latter, and they and the preparation of the same are paid for **in full by** this agreement.

Said Volk, further for said consideration **agrees to** furnish all **working** plans, drawings, designs and specifications, and copies **thereof, and** models which may be required for the architectural and other work named in specifications No. 1, and all work specified in **specifications Nos. 2 and 3** (said specifications having been already prepared by said Volk), needed and required **for the** execution of the work herein named, and also all other **specifications,** plans, drawings, etc., required for the completion **of said** monument in accordance with the existing general **design thereof.**

Said Volk further agrees for said consideration **to superintend** the work named in specifications Nos. 1, 2 and 3 as the same may be contracted for and directed by said Commissioners to **be done,** and all other work in and about **the** completion **of said monument** and its grounds, if and as requested and directed by **said Commissioners.** The superintending of said Volk to be strictly under the direction of said Commission, **and** no authority **being hereby given** to said Volk to incur **any** liability for and on account of **said Commissioners, or make any change** in said work not authorized by them **without their specific assent.**

And **in** consideration of the faithful performance of the foregoing, the said Commissioners of the Douglas Monument at Chicago hereby agree to pay to said Leonard W Volk the sum of **five** hundred dollars. In witness whereof the parties hereto have subscribed these presents (the party **of first part** by its President and Secretary) the day and year first above written.

Commissioners of Douglas Monument at Chicago, by

J. D. CATON, *Pres.*
M. W. FULLER, *Sec'y.*
LEONARD W. VOLK.

The writer subsequently rebated $200 from the above contract.

At the next meeting of the committee, the writer was ordered to omit certain ornaments resting on the corners of the main base of the superstructure, **and** enlarge the diameter of the column at the top, when the following advertisement was published in the daily papers:

DOUGLAS MONUMENT COMMISSION.

Proposals are invited for the New England granite work necessary to complete the Douglas Monument in Chicago, and for walls, sidewalk and limestone or sandstone coping,

Also for marble and tile work in the tomb chamber and work on sarcophagus.

Full plans and specifications of the work can be seen at the office of Robert T. Lincoln, No 31 Portland Block, Chicago.

The above work is described in three separate specifications, and proposals are requested for the work on each specification separately, and also for all the work together. Specimens of the material proposed must accompany each bid.

Each bidder will name in his proposal the time within which **he** will complete the work proposed for by him, if his bid is accepted.

A satisfactory bond, with two sureties, in the sum of one-half the amount of each contract, will be required of the successful bidder, to insure the completion of such contract. Names of proposed sureties should accompany bids.

No payments will be made on any contract until the full completion of the work named.

Proposals should be in sealed envelopes, marked "Proposals for Work on Douglas Monument," and addressed to Melville W. Fuller, Secretary of the Commission, No. 152 Dearborn street, Chicago.

Proposals will be received until ten o'clock in the morning of Saturday, July 28, 1877, and will be opened at a meeting of the Commission.

The right is reserved to accept or reject any bid, or to reject all bids, in the absolute discretion of the Commission.

Chicago, July 18, 1877.

ROBERT T. LINCOLN,
POTTER PALMER,
MELVILLE W. FULLER,
Committee.

The meeting was held as advertised and **the bids of a large number of contractors were opened.**

The superstructure was **let to** one of the lowest bidders

at $15,600, to be of Hallowell, Maine, granite, and was completed July, 1878.

The limestone work, consisting of the copings, sidewalk and terrace wall, was let shortly after at $4984, and was completed in sixty days.

In October, the writer was commissioned to execute a colossal statue of Douglas, in bronze, to surmount the monument, as appears by—

This agreement, made this 17th day of October, A. D. 1877, between the Commissioners to complete the Douglas Monument at Chicago, of the first part, and Leonard W. Volk, of the city of Chicago, county of Cook and State of Illinois, of the second part, witnesseth:

That the said Leonard W. Volk, for the consideration hereinafter mentioned, agrees to execute for the Douglas Monument at Chicago, Illinois, to the satisfaction of the party of the first part, a colossal statue of Stephen A. Douglas, in standard bronze metal, not less than nine feet high, to be a faithful and true likeness of said Douglas both in feature and in form throughout, and place it on the column of the monument as designed, by the first day of June, A. D. 1878.

And said Volk also agrees that the model for said statue shall be exhibited to said party of the first part, and that the party of the first part shall be informed of the formula adopted by said Volk for the bronze metal, and that said party of the first part shall be satisfied with the execution of the model and with the formula adopted before the casting of the statue is attempted.

In consideration whereof, the said party of the first part agrees to pay the said L. W. Volk, upon the completion of the statue as aforesaid, of the likeness and material aforesaid, and the placing of the same in positon and acceptance thereof by said party of the first part, the sum of eight thousand dollars ($8,000).

In witness whereof, the parties hereto have subscribed these presents (the party of the first part by its President and Secretary thereunto duly authorized), the day and year above written.

THE COMMISSIONERS TO COMPLETE THE
DOUGLAS MONUMENT AT CHICAGO,
BY J. D. CATON, *President.*
M. W. FULLER, *Secretary.*
LEONARD W. VOLK.

Soon after, it was decided by the Commissioners to remove the **limestone** tomb or substructure built twelve years before and **rebuild it of** granite, utilizing the old ashler facing for the inner **walls.** Some changes were made by reducing the diameter of the tomb at the top, and omitting the arches which connected the octagonally formed buttrass-pedestals at the four corners of tomb with **the cornice,** substituting **square ones** about half the height, and making **a** square door-way instead of the keyed arch. The foundations **as** originally constructed were examined **by** experts but were not disturbed.

On Dec. 31, 1877, the contract for the renovated substruct**ure was** let to the lowest bidders at $7893, and is of "Fox Island" Maine granite, and was completed in June, 1878.

The statue of Douglas was hoisted into position as soon as the capstone of the column was placed. **And** was informally unveiled July **17th, in presence** of several of the Commission**ers,** the only sister of **Senator** Douglas, **Mrs.** Granger, who came from her home at Clifton Springs, **New** York, to view the work, and a considerable number of spectators.

The following remarks were made by Judge **Caton upon the** occasion:

"As a representative of **the** Commission appointed by the State Legislature to execute its purpose in the completion of the monument for Senator Douglas, it is proper for me to say that we are gratified to see so many appear here to witness the manner in which this work has been done. We have assembled here,—the Commission,—not for the purpose of a public exhibition in any manner or form, or in any sense of the word; but for the purpose of examining how the work thus far has been executed. It has now progressed to that stage when you can see, and we can see, the form and features of the monument erected in honor of Judge Douglas, and we deem it proper that the Commission should **meet** here, for the purpose of examining the manner in which this work **has** been executed; and I repeat, that it is a matter of gratification **to** see so many of **the** citizens of Chicago spontaneously met here with us for the same purpose. I may be permitted to say, that the completion of this work—so far as the monument proper and the statute are concerned, it is completed,—I may, I say, be permitted to say that the completion of this work is an era in the history of our State, which, some of us at least, can sensibly feel. Seventeen years ago, Judge Douglas was taken from among us. At that time his features were familiar to almost every man, woman and child in Illinois. Since that time a new generation has grown up, strangers to his features.

They all knew the sound of his voice which electrified the multitude; they knew the expression of his countenance whence beamed that light which lit up the great multitudes of people. During the meantime, many of these have passed away, and a new generation has come, who will to-day for the first time look upon the countenance of which they had only heard. Standing as I do in this position, it is proper to say, that but few comparatively, of the contemporaries of Judge Douglas are left; the most distinguished of them have been swept away, one by one; and why a few of us of lesser light should have been spared, none but Omnipotence can tell. How long we shall follow in his footsteps of course is hidden in the future.

We return to you our thanks for your kind attendance. I will now proceed to uncover the statue, that all may look on the features which all so much loved."

In August, the writer entered into the following agreement to execute the four heroic size symbolical statues for the pedestals at each corner of the tomb.

This agreement, made this 7th day of August, A. D. 1878, between the Commissioners to complete the Douglas Monument at Chicago, of the first part, and Leonard W. Volk, of the city of Chicago, county of Cook, and State of Illinois, of the second part, witnesseth:

That the said L. W. Volk, for the consideration hereinafter mentioned, agrees to execute for the Douglas Monument at Chicago, Illinois, to the satisfaction of the party of the first part, four statues representing " Illinois," " History," " Justice" and " Eloquence," in standard bronze metal, not less than seven feet high, if standing, but to be in sitting posture, each, and place the same upon four pedestals at the four corners of the substructure of said monument by the 1st day of May, A. D. 1879.

And said Volk also agrees that the model for each of said statues shall be exhibited to said party of the first part, and that said party of the first part shall be informed of the formula adopted by said Volk for the bronze metal, and that said party of the first part shall be satisfied with the execution of the model and with the formula adopted before the casting of either of the said statues is attempted.

In consideration whereof, **the said party of the first part** agrees to pay the said L. W. Volk, upon the completion of each of the four statues aforesaid of the material aforesaid, and the placing of the same in position and acceptance thereof by said party of the first part, **the sum of sixteen hundred and** twenty-five dollars, being the sum of six thousand five hundred dollars for said four statues when completed, placed in position and accepted as aforesaid.

In witness whereof, the parties hereto have subscribed these presents (the party of the first part by its president and secretary thereunto duly authorized) the day and year above written.

THE COMMISSIONERS TO COMPLETE THE
DOUGLAS MONUMENT AT CHICAGO,
(Signed)　　　　　By J. D. CATON, *Pres.*
(Signed)　　　　　M. W. FULLER, *Sec'y,*
(Signed)　　　　　LEONARD W. VOLK.

I, Melville W. Fuller, of Chicago, the Secretary of the Commissioners to complete the Douglas Monument at Chicago, do hereby certify that the foregoing is a correct copy of the contract for four statues entered into between said Commissioners and L. W. Volk, and voted May 1st, 1878. **As witness** my hand this 8th day of August, A. D. 1878.

MELVILLE W. FULLER,
Sec'y Commissioners to complete Douglas Monument at Chicago.

Upon the assembling of the legislature in the winter of 1879, the Commissioners forwarded their report to the Governor, stating the amounts expended from the appropriation of $50,000 and liability under **contract for** symbolical statues; and that in order to complete the four bas-reliefs as originally designed for the panels of the base of superstructure, and also to **substitute granite in** place of the old limestone steps or base of substructure, $9,000 additional to the $50,000 would be required.

Governor Cullom in his message recommended that this sum be appropriated for the **purpose.**

The following bill was introduced in the House by Mr. Moses Wentworth, and was in due time **passed.**

An act to appropriate nine thousand ($9,000) dollars for the **completion of the** Douglas Monument at Chicago. **That said Commission was** compelled **to remove and rebuild** the substructure thereof, requiring an expenditure not anticipated **at the time of** the passage of the act creating said Commission, and necessitating a further appropriation; therefore,

Be it enacted, by the people of the State **of** Illinois, represented **in** the General Assembly, That the **sum** of nine thousand **($9,000)** dollars be, and the same is hereby appropriated for the completion of said monument, and the Auditor of Public Accounts is hereby authorized and directed to draw his warrant on **the** State Treasurer for said amount out of money not otherwise appropriated, upon the certificate **of a** majority of said Commissioners, **from** time to time, as the same may **be** needed.

The same bill was presented **to the Senate by** Mr. Bash, who in a **speech** advocating **its** passage explained the reasons for the appropriation. It **was defeated; whereupon** Senator De Lany **moved a** re-consideration. The **vote** resulted in a tie. Lieut. Gov. Shuman, the presiding officer, voted in favor of re-consideration, **and** the discussion of the bill was then resumed, **which** was amended, making the amount $5,000, and **then it was** moved to refer it to committee on appropriations. **Lost. The** Senate again refused to order it to a third reading by a vote of 21 to 22.

Just before the **adjournment in May, ex-member of the House** of Representatives, Hon. Jos. E. Smith, who introduced the original bill, proceeded to Springfield and succeeded in getting the House bill which had gone to **Senate** committee on appropriations resurrected, and it was shortly afterwards passed by **the Senate** and approved by the Governor May 27th, 1879.

About July 22d, **the first of** the four **statues,** representing Illinois, was successfully placed upon its pedestal, and on September 28th the second, History, was put in position.

About December 30th, 1879, the third, Justice, was completed and seated safely upon its pedestal.

On July 24th, 1879, the Executive Committee of the Board of Commissioners issued an advertisement inviting proposals to complete in granite the circular bases or steps around the tomb in place of the limestone. Three, instead of the seven original steps, and curtailment of diameter eight feet and four inches, having been previously determined upon, the contract was in due time let to the lowest bidder at $3,925, and completed March, 1880. All the granite work was cut at the quarries in Maine.

On March 1st of same year the last contract was made with the writer to execute the four *Bas-reliefs* as follows:

This agreement, made this 9th day of March, A. D. 1880, between the Commissioners to complete the Douglas Monument at Chicago, of the first part, and L. W. Volk, of the city of Chicago, County of Cook, and State of Illinois of the second part, Witnesseth: That the said L. W. Volk for the consideration hereinafter mentioned, agrees to execute to the satisfaction of the party of the first part, four Bas-reliefs in standard bronze metal, for the four panels on the main base of the superstructure of the Douglas Monument at Chicago, and to place the same in position, all to be done to the satisfaction of the said party of the first part, by the first day of January A. D. 1881. And said Volk also agrees that the design as well as the model for each of said Bas-reliefs shall be exhibited to said party of the first part, and that said party of the first part shall be informed of the formula adopted by said Volk for the bronze metal, that said party of the first part shall be satisfied with the design as well as the execution of the model, and with the formula adopted, before the casting of either of the said Bas-reliefs is attempted.

In consideration whereof the said party of the first part agrees to pay the said L. W. Volk, upon the completion of each of the Bas-reliefs aforesaid, of the material aforesaid, and the placing of the same in position and acceptance thereof by said party of the first part, the sum of twelve hundred dollars, being the sum of four thousand eight hundred dollars for said four Bas-reliefs when completed, placed in position and accepted as aforesaid.

In witness whereof, the parties hereto have subscribed these presents (the party of the first part by its committee thereunto duly authorized) the day and year above written.

COMMISSIONERS TO COMPLETE THE
DOUGLAS MONUMENT AT CHICAGO,
BY POTTER PALMER,
LYMAN TRUMBULL,
M. W. FULLER,
ROBERT T. LINCOLN,
Committee.
LEONARD W. VOLK.

The last of the statues of the monument, representing Eloquence, was safely placed May 13th, 1880. All these statues, including **the** Douglas, were first modeled in clay by **the** writer, in Chicago, and approved by the commissioners; then cast **in** Plaster of Paris, and in **that** material forwarded to the bronze foundry **of M. J. Power, New York, who** has cast them in the **best bronze** metal, *i. e.:* **90 parts copper,** 8 parts tin, and **2 parts zinc.**

The statue of Douglas, which is 9 feet 9 inches high, weighs **about 2200 pounds.** The four symbolical statues, if standing in upright posture, would be about 7 feet 6 inches high, **and** average weight of each is about 1150 pounds.

DESCRIPTION AND DIMENSIONS OF THE MONUMENT **AS COMPLETED.**

The octagonal base coping, of **Lemont,** Ill., Limestone, **is** 70 feet in diameter. The first **of the three** circular bases of the substructure is 42 feet 2 **inches in** diameter, and the height **of the three** together is 4 feet 3 inches. The tomb is octagonally **formed, 20 feet 3** inches in diameter, and 10 feet high, **to** the plinth-base **of superstructure.** Its chamber is 8 feet 9 inches square **by** 7 feet 2 inches high. The pedestal at each of the four corners of **the tomb is** 6 feet high, with **base 4 feet 2 inches** square. The octagonally formed pedestal of the superstructure above the tomb is 18 feet 10 inches **high, to** the circular **base** of the column. Its plinth-base is 15 feet in diameter. The **length of** the column, including its base, which is 2 feet thick, **is** 46 feet 5 inches, and is 5 feet 2 inches in diameter at base, with a diameter of 3 feet 6 inches at the top. The cap, including the ornamented frieze, is 4 feet 6 inches high, and the statue-base above is 2 feet high, making the entire height of the monument, including the statue, 95 feet 9 inches. The ornamentation cut in the granite consists of a wreath and the letter "D" on the lintel of the tomb door. There are raised shields on the corners of the main base of superstructure, the pedestal of which is ornamented with festoons and wreaths of laurel, and *flambeaux* on the octagonal corners—all in high *bas-relief*.

The two main sections of the column are marked by belts of raised stars, indicating the number of states; and the frieze of the cap is encircled with oak leaves in high relief.

Within the tomb-chamber repose the remains of Senator Douglas, **in** an iron casket which is placed **in** a white marble sarcophagus, lined with lead. The following inscription **is lettered on the** front side:

"STEPHEN A. DOUGLAS,

"BORN APRIL 23D, 1813. DIED JUNE 3D, 1861.

"**Tell my children to obey the laws** and uphold the Constitution."

The marble of the sarcophagus is from his native State and county—Rutland, Vermont. The tomb has a heavy wrought-iron grated door, with padlock, and an inner iron safe-door with combination lock. The entire superstructure of the monument is made of solid blocks of granite except the die of pedestal, which is in four parts, and has a small hollow space within, containing the copper box of records, coins, etc., which was deposited in the corner-stone of the original limestone **tomb.**

The faces of the raised **shields,** stars **and panels** are polished or glossed.

THE BRONZE STATUARY.

The colossal statue of Douglas surmounting the top of the column, looking eastward over the lake, is 9 feet 9 inches high, and represents him standing in repose, with scroll in left hand pressed against the hip, and the right hand thrust under the lapel of his tightly buttoned under-coat.

The four pedestals at the base are occupied by heroic-size statues representing Illinois, History, Justice and Eloquence, in sitting attitudes; the former has her right hand placed on the State coat of arms, with ears of corn in her left hand, and crowned with a chaplet of wheat, and is supposed to be in the act of relating the story of the State to History, on the opposite corner, who, with *stylus* in hand, is about to record it upon the scroll lying across her lap; her left foot rests upon a pile of tablets.

Justice rests her right hand upon a sheathed sword, and holds the balances in her left. Eloquence points with her right hand towards the statue of Douglas, while the left rests upon a lyrical instrument.

All these statues are differently composed and robed in harmonious and classical garments.

The four *Bas-reliefs* in the panels of the main base of superstructure represent the advance of civilization in America, first by an Aboriginal Indian scene in which appears the sun rising above the horizon of a lake, upon which two Indians are about to embark in a canoe; wigwams, with squaws and papoose, and an elder and two younger Indians, and a dog, the elder in the act of shooting a deer with bow and arrow.

The second represents Pioneer Settlers building log cabin, plowing, sowing grain, and a group of mother, children and dog resting before the unfinished cabin and the "Prairie Schooner" wagon.

In the third scene Commerce and Enterprise are represented,

by trackmen working on the railroad, a locomotive, vessels discharging and receiving merchandise, an elevator warehouse and telegraph line. The fourth and last of the scenes illustrates Education—the culmination of civilization.

THE MONUMENT GROUND

Is bounded on the north by Woodland Park with frontage of 260 feet.

On the east by the Illinois Central Railway and lake Michigan, with frontage of 300 feet. On the south by Douglas avenue or 35th street, with a frontage of 402 feet.

And on the west by an alley, and the width of the lot along this alley is 266 feet.

RECAPITULATION OF THE COST OF THE GROUND AND MONUMENT.

The ground—State appropriation	$25,000
Foundations and limestone tomb—Public subscriptions	12,350
Drafting and superintendence—State appropriation	300
Limestone copings, sidewalk and terrace wall—State appropriation	4,984
Superstructure, Hallowell granite—State appropriation	15,600
Substructure, four pedestals and tomb, Fox Island granite—State appropriation	7,893
Statue of Douglas, in bronze metal—State appropriation	8,000
Statues of Illinois, History, Justice and Eloquence, in bronze metal—State appropriation	6,500
Three base-steps around tomb, Fox Island granite—State appropriation	3,925
Four Bas-reliefs, in bronze metal—State appropriation	4,800
Miscellaneous expenses—grading and gardening done and to be done—State appropriation	6,998
Total expense of the Douglas Monument	$96,350

Douglas's Cottage, and the Registry for Visitors to the Monument, are numbered **36** Douglas Avenue, adjacent to the Monument Grounds.

www.ingramcontent.com/pod-product-compliance
Lightning Source LLC
Chambersburg PA
CBHW021936160426
43195CB00011B/1113